Stefano Corbo

NOTES FROM THE UNDER

WORLD

An Architectural Exploration

SCHIFFER PUBLISHING
4880 Lower Valley Road • Atglen, PA 19310

Other Schiffer Books on Related Subjects:
Housing and the City: Love vs. Hope, Daniel Solomon,
ISBN 978-0-7643-5643-8
Designing for Disaster, Boyce Thompson, 978-0-7643-5784-8
Anatomy of a Great Home, Boyce Thompson,
ISBN 978-0-7643-5465-6

Library of Congress Control Number: 2019934834

Edited by Cheryl Weber
Designed by Molly Shields
Type set in Gotham/Georgia

ISBN: 978-0-7643-5840-1
Printed in China

Published by Schiffer Publishing, Ltd.
4880 Lower Valley Road
Atglen, PA 19310
Phone: (610) 593-1777; Fax: (610) 593-2002
E-mail: Info@schifferbooks.com
Web: www.schifferbooks.com

For our complete selection of fine books on this and related subjects, please visit our website at www.schifferbooks.com. You may also write for a free catalog.

Schiffer Publishing's titles are available at special discounts for bulk purchases for sales promotions or premiums. Special editions, including personalized covers, corporate imprints, and excerpts, can be created in large quantities for special needs. For more information, contact the publisher.

We are always looking for people to write books on new and related subjects. If you have an idea for a book, please contact us at proposals@schifferbooks.com.

Contents

Hoc Schema exprimit Caloris sive Ignis nidos, vel quod idem est, pyrophylacia per universa Geocosmi viscera admirando DEI opificio, varie dist
tantopere foret necessarium; Nemo autem sibi persuadeat Ignem revera hoc pacto quo schema refert, constitutum esse; eoque prorsus ordine dispos
quisnam illuc penetravit unquam ex hominibus? Hoc itaque Schemate solummodo ostendere voluimus, Telluris viscera plena esse æstu
alio, disposita sint. Ex centro igitur Ignem per omnes Subterrestris mundi semitas usque ad ipsos exterioris superficiei mon
A litera. Reliqua sunt æstuaria Naturæ, signata B. Canales pyragogi C. minimi vero rivi sunt fissuræ Terræ, per q

Acknowledgments

This book wouldn't have been possible without the support of those who shared their photographic archive. My thanks go to Cinzia Solimene, from Ceramica Artistica Solimene; Bruce Townsley and his Missile Silo house; Bruno Despierre, from B-ILD Architects; Biancoshock and Veronica Barria; David Closes and photographer Jordi Surroca; Lola Botia, from Fernando Higueras Foundation; Oving Architekten and Susan Schuls; Marc Maurer United Architects; Andrea Huwyler-Bachmann, from Sonnenberg Bunker; Pekka Leskelä, from HKP Architects; Claudio Lucchin & Architetti Associati; Albert France-Lanord Architects; Peter Šenk, at Studio Stratum; Lori Kharpoutlian, at DW5 / Bernard Khoury; Bethany Thurston, at Growing Underground; Martie Steyn, from AngloGold Ashanti; and Director Daniele Maruca and Shino Kobayashi, at the Feuerle Collection.

Thanks to the Department of Interior Architecture at RISD (Rhode Island School of Design), and to the department head, Liliane Wong, who allowed me to apply some of these ideas to a design studio I taught. I'm also grateful to RISD student assistant Mingyi Hu for her invaluable help with Chinese vernacular architecture.

Fig. 0.01. Athanasius Kircher's *Mundus subterraneus, quo universae denique naturae divitiae*, 1665. Illustration of underground fire canals.

Introduction

In 1638, seven years after Mount Vesuvius erupted, the Jesuit scholar Athanasius Kircher traveled to Naples and climbed the volcano that had just caused the death of more than 4,000 people. After descending into the crater to measure the temperature, Kircher reported:

> *I thought I beheld the habitation of Hell, wherein nothing seemed to be much wanting besides the horrid fantasms and apparitions of Devils. . . . I heard horrible bellowings and roarings, and there was an unexpressible stink. . . . The smoke and fire and stench continually belch'd forth out of eleven several places, and made me in like manner belch, and as it were, vomit back again, at it.*[1]

His encounter with the brutal and tumultuous Mount Vesuvius piqued his curiosity and inspired his further explorations of Earth's interior. This culminated in the famous *Mundus subterraneus*, a comprehensive, twelve-volume atlas published between 1665 and 1678. *Mundus subterraneus* expresses Kircher's belief in an interconnected subterranean world with a mysterious system of arteries that reaches the center of the globe—a mass of flame sending heat to the surface through channels and fissures. Fascinating maps support this hypothesis: mountains, oceans, and volcanos are described as visible manifestations of this incessant magmatic flow (fig. 0.01).

Despite some of his unscientific theories, Kircher is credited with providing an exhaustive description of the world where water, fire, sun, moon, fossils, and even lost islands obey the same general logic. At the same time, *Mundus subterraneus* was an attempt to satisfy the curiosity of a large, erudite audience. Over the centuries, in fact, the idea of an underground world populated by invisible forces has fueled the fantasy of artists, scholars, and scientists. From the myth of Orpheus and Eurydice, to Plato's Allegory of the Cave, to Dante's exploration of Hell, mythology, literature, and the underground have often overlain and morphed into unique narratives. At the root of this fascination are two things: on the one hand, the subterranean is associated with fear and danger—the domain of evil. On the other hand, it is also seen as an oasis for freedom and imagination. As Kircher showed, the subterranean symbolized thirst for knowledge, fear of the unknown, and the will to push the boundaries of human intelligence.

In the realm of architecture and design, humans have explored the space below their feet for different purposes: to flee persecution and war, to find protection from severe weather, and to improve city life.

By carving, digging, hiding, and unveiling, many different kinds of structures have been built over time: bunkers, catacombs, aqueducts, and, more recently, dwellings, data centers, and seed banks. This book aims to cover the history of such spaces under a general definition: the Underworld. My premise is that the Underworld is a broad interpretative category that includes but is not limited to subterranean examples. It reaches beyond its most immediate and literal interpretation and includes architecture whose internal functioning is not completely revealed, or whose spatial articulation is based on a relationship of visible and invisible elements.

Furthermore, underground spaces belong to the Underworld, but the Underworld is not always belowground: it can be inaccessible or far from prying eyes, yet located in the urban core. The Underworld manifests itself not as a specific physical condition, but in the role it plays in a particular context. Despite their qualities, these spaces have an indirect but relevant impact on the built environment. In other words, the Underworld is but an invisible extension both of historical and contemporary architectural production.

The fascination with the deep unknown as described in literature sometimes distracts us from the essence of these secret spaces: that they are formed by the same economic and cultural forces as visible architecture. Global phenomena such as migrations, epidemics, and wars have always had a clear correlation to the Underworld. Because of their unstable nature, underworld spaces are constantly evolving, and we will explore their evolution in relation to the outside world in more than eighty projects from different eras and in different geographic locations. The following five chapters offer lenses through which to understand the Underworld's physical and symbolic relevance.

UPSIDE DOWN: THE MAKING OF THE CITY

Since the first urban settlements, the Underworld has been an inexhaustible source of exploitation. Mining, for example, is one of the most extreme examples of the Underworld: to extract fossil fuels, metals, and minerals, the underground has been continually eroded by tunnels and work areas. This required a huge technological effort, and the outcome was a unique microcosm physically separated from the aboveground world but also deeply tied to its economy.

In addition to mines, a parallel universe composed of aqueducts, cemeteries, and sewers runs beneath the city surface and has guaranteed its functioning over the centuries. The exploitation of the Underworld for economic and engineering purposes continues today in new architectural forms. The need for secure storage for computer systems, internet servers, and IT operations has produced the rise of new, mysterious structures—so-called data centers. This chapter will explore old and new infrastructures by deconstructing the city to reveal its inaccessible spaces.

DESIGN AS WARFARE

An intriguing perspective on the Underworld comes from the military complex. If during World War II anti-raid shelters represented a rudimentary yet successful solution to protecting citizens from massive bombing operations, in recent times the fear of nuclear attacks has led many countries to rethink their defense systems. All around the world, not only were fallout bunkers and tunnels built, but also complex underground cities that could accommodate thousands of people in wartime. While some of these projects were designed to double as military structures and as public facilities in peacetime, today most of these spaces have been simply abandoned and closed off to the public, their destiny uncertain. However, there are some exceptions. This chapter will present examples of bunkers turned into tourist attractions—monuments to the Cold War—and tunnels converted into museums and art galleries. In other cases, these historic structures have been preserved and incorporated into national parks and reserves.

LIFE AND DEATH IN THE UNDERWORLD

Subterranean settlements can be found everywhere, from Cappadocia, Turkey; to Matera, Italy; to China with its sunken courtyards, and many are examples of vernacular dwellings. Nature is carved out to achieve favorable living conditions, especially in response to extreme weather. All these examples prove the existence of an anonymous and collective intelligence—in contrast to the individual act of the artist-genius—capable of producing remarkable architecture despite scarce resources.

Historically, the Underworld also symbolized the bridge between life and death. Over the centuries, sacred spaces and catacombs have been built underground, providing shelter for those escaping religious persecution. Today we face a renewed interest in subterranean ways of living. On the one hand, the economic elite has begun to install swimming pools, billiard rooms, car parks, and even tennis courts in the basements of their elegant houses. In London, for example, between 2008 and 2012 permission was granted for more than 800 subterranean excavations in the Kensington and Chelsea neighborhoods.[2] On the other hand, growing environmental concerns are prompting architects to root their projects in nature—an attempt to live in harmony with the earth.

EMERGING FROM DARKNESS

As urban developers continue to erect new buildings, an opposite phenomenon is going on: abandoned structures once belonging to an invisible urban network are being turned into public facilities and finally given back to the community. Reemerging from an unseen past, these buildings are officially being absorbed into the urban fabric. This process of adaptive reuse offers a wide range of examples: caves converted into post offices, industrial silos into houses or art centers, medieval churches into bookstores. In this way, design becomes a progressive process of unveiling.

ON NATURE AND ARTIFICE

The Underworld is not only the expression of a hidden universe. It can also be a hybrid of components: nature and culture, architecture and city, and so forth. For example, nature does not just mean the presence of greenery. Nature can be artificial—in other words, it's possible to reproduce nature in vitro. From the construction of monastic structures carved out of the mountain, to biophilic design experiments, to buildings that seem to merge with the landscape, nature is not only represented, it is incorporated into complex environments.

By dissecting the Underworld in these five spheres, this book aims to prove that despite their differences, both exterior architectural expression and its invisible counterpart are produced by the same agents and dynamics. In other words, the exterior built environment is but a visible expression of a broader scenario, in which visible and invisible elements are intertwined. Once we make this connection, a counterhistory of architecture can finally be written.

ILLUSTRATED SITES AT A GLANCE

CHAPTER 1

1 Victoria Embankment, London
2 Mponeng Gold Mine, South Africa
3 Wieliczka Salt Mine, Poland
4 Piscina Mirabilis, Italy
5 Basilica Cistern, Istanbul
6 Chand Baori, India
7 Old Newgate, Connecticut
8 Breda Panopticon, Netherlands
9 IOR Bank, Rome
10 RÉSO Montreal
11 Canary Wharf, London
12 Bratislava Metro, Slovakia
13 Cincinnati Subway, Ohio
14 Cobble Hill Tunnel, New York
15 Telefónica Data Center, Madrid
16 White Mountain Data Center, Stockholm
17 Svalbard Global Seed Vault, Norway

CHAPTER 2

1 Moscow Metro-2, Russia
2 Pyongyang Metro, North Korea
3 Dixia Cheng, China
4 Librairie Avant-Garde, China
5 Titan Missile Museum, Arizona
6 Missile Silo House, Texas
7 Dupont Underground, Washington, DC
8 Gaza Tunnels, Palestine
9 Sonnenberg Bunker, Switzerland
10 Itäkeskus pools, Finland
11 Feuerle Collection, Berlin
12 Bunker 599, Netherlands
13 Bunker Pavilion, Netherlands

CHAPTER 3

1 Mesa Verde, Colorado
2 Derinkuyu, Turkey
3 Kaymakli, Turkey
4 Sassi, Italy
5 Pantalica, Sicily
6 Guadix Cave Houses, Spain
7 Matmata, Tunisia
8 Yaodong, China
9 San Gennaro Catacombs, Italy
10 Fontanelle Cemetery, Italy
11 Paris Catacombs
12 Changling Tomb, Beijing
13 Dingling Tomb, Beijing
14 Rascainfiernos, Madrid
15 Gilardi House, Mexico
16 La Fábrica, Spain

CHAPTER 4

1 Zeitz MOCAA, Capetown, South Africa
2 Shenzhen Silo, China
3 Palais de Tokyo, Paris
4 Quai de la Fosse, France
5 Westerbork Camp, Netherlands
6 Netherlands Institute for Sound and Vision
7 Castelgrande, Bellinzona, Switzerland
8 Maritime Museum of Denmark
9 Hannah Arendt School, Italy
10 B018, Beirut
11 Postojna Post Office, Slovenia
12 Selexyz Bookstore, Netherlands
13 Sant Francesc Church, Spain
14 Abbey of Our Lady of Nový Dvůr, Czech Republic

CHAPTER 5

1 Longmen Grottoes, China
2 Bet Giyorgis Church, Ethiopia
3 Coober Pedy Church, Australia
4 Monastery of Hozoviotissa, Greece
5 Temppeliaukio Church, Helsinki
6 Mirador, Lanzarote, Canary Islands
7 Antinori Winery, Tuscany
8 Solimene Factory, Italy
9 Paul Klee Museum, Switzerland
10 Growing Underground Farm, London
11 Truffle House, Spain

Fig. 0.02. The Underworld map. *Courtesy of Stefano Corbo, 2018*

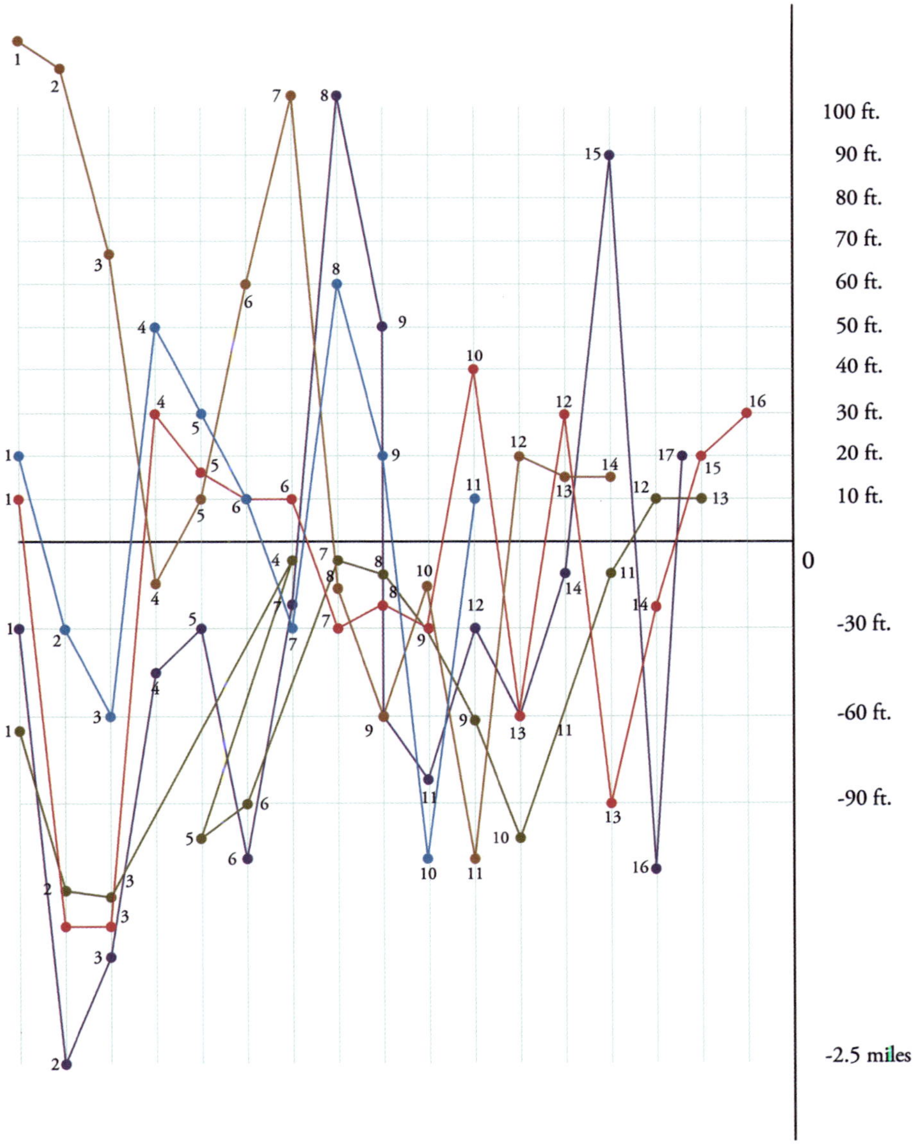

Fig. 0.03. Heights and depths of Underworld illustrated sites. *Courtesy of Stefano Corbo, 2018*

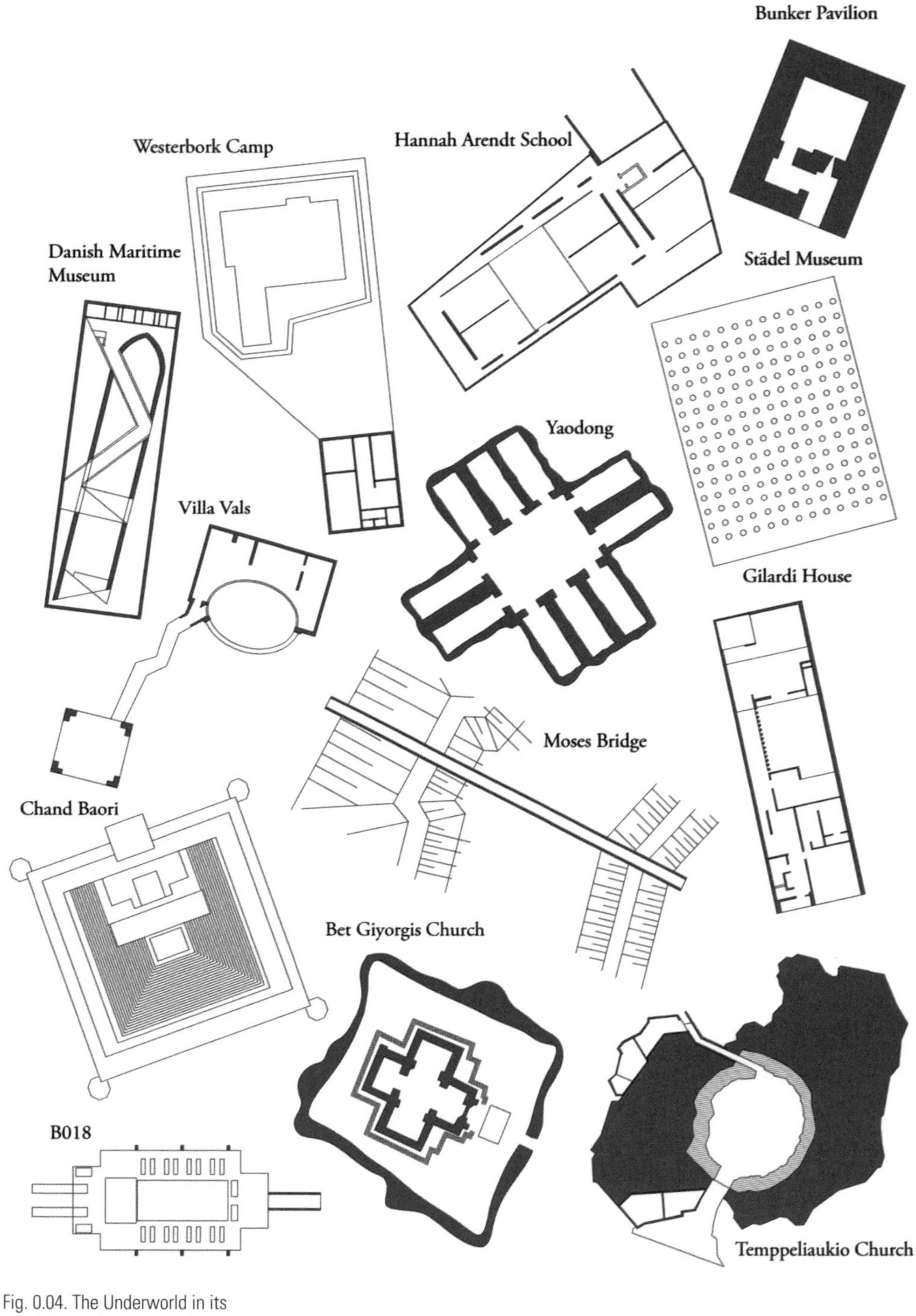

Fig. 0.04. The Underworld in its multiple manifestations. *Courtesy of Stefano Corbo, 2018*

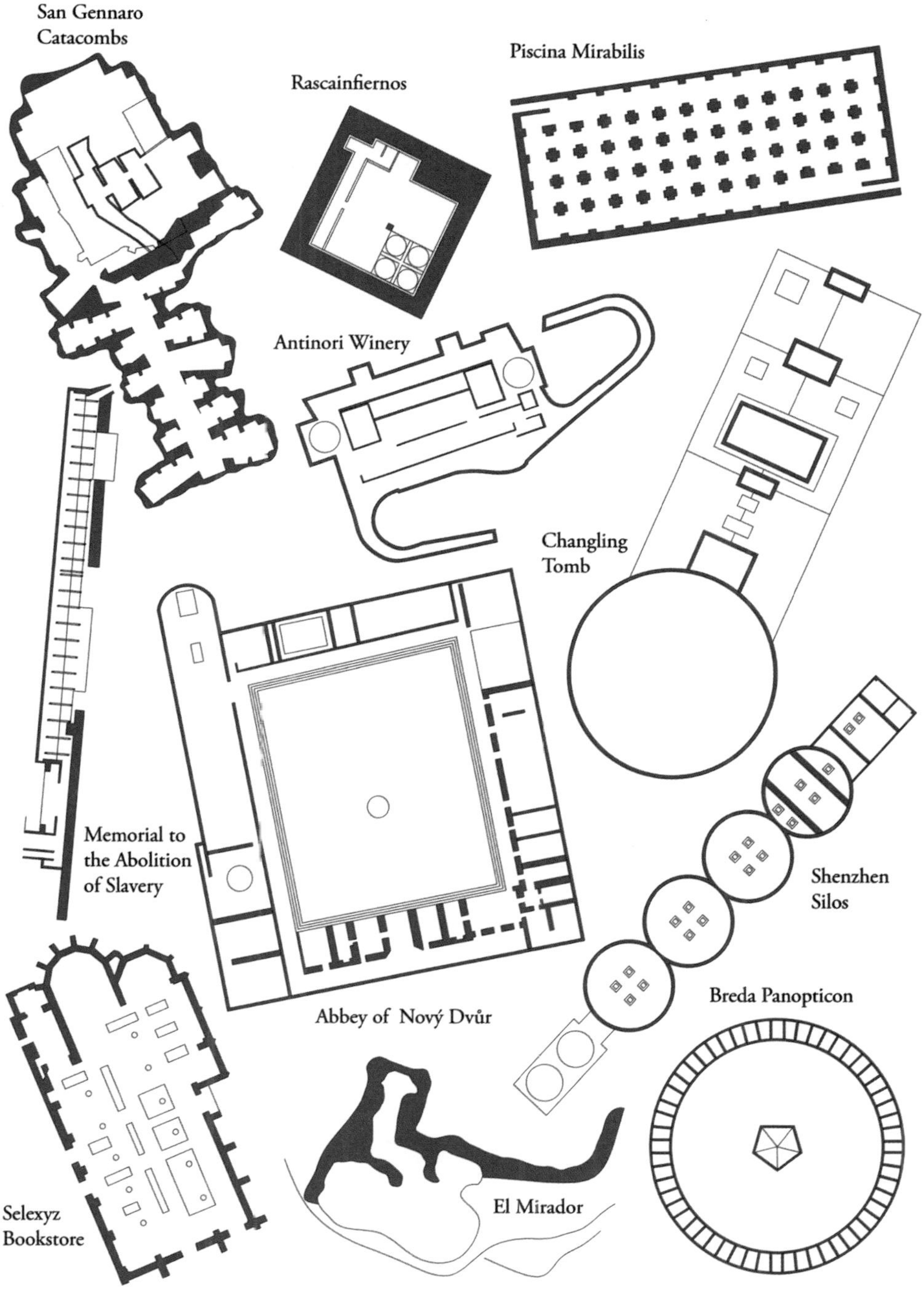
San Gennaro
Catacombs
Rascainfiernos
Piscina Mirabilis
Antinori Winery
Changling
Tomb
Memorial to
the Abolition
of Slavery
Shenzhen
Silos
Abbey of Nový Dvůr
Breda Panopticon
El Mirador
Selexyz
Bookstore

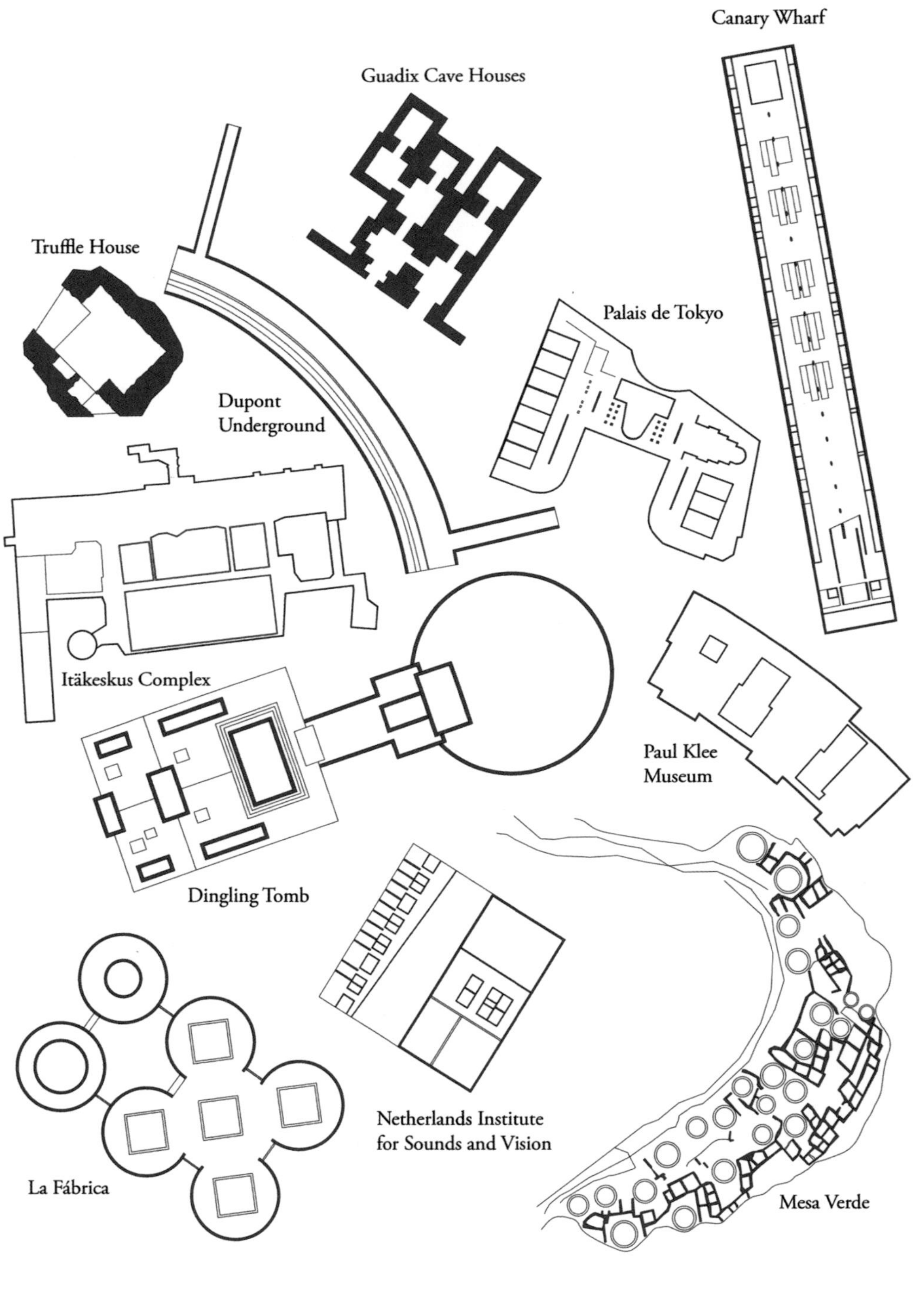
Canary Wharf
Guadix Cave Houses
Truffle House
Palais de Tokyo
Dupont
Underground
Itäkeskus Complex
Paul Klee
Museum
Dingling Tomb
Netherlands Institute
for Sounds and Vision
La Fábrica
Mesa Verde

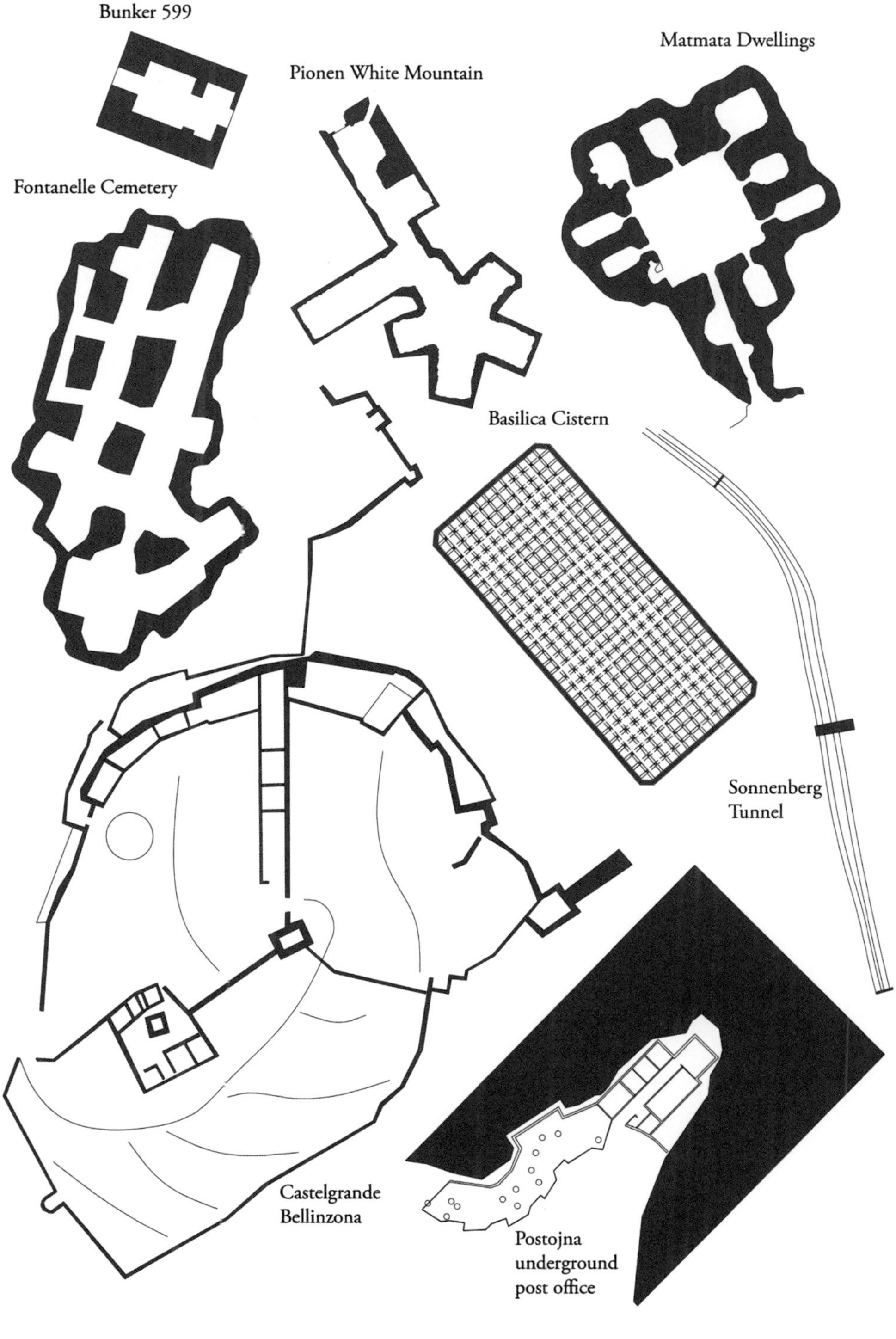
Bunker 599
Pionen White Mountain
Matmata Dwellings
Fontanelle Cemetery
Basilica Cistern
Sonnenberg
Tunnel
Castelgrande
Bellinzona
Postojna
underground
post office

ONE

UPSIDE DOWN

The Making of the City

In the second half of the nineteenth century, impressive works of civil engineering were built in London, similar to what was happening in Paris and other European capitals. This development radically altered not only its urban fabric but also its image. The Thames Embankment, for example, consisting of three districts—the Victoria, Chelsea, and Albert Embankments—was a multistory subterranean structure that incorporated a new sewage system and an underground railway to relieve traffic congestion. The modern network of sewers was prompted by chronic cholera outbreaks in 1832, 1849, and 1854. Although the idea of an embankment was not new—it had been proposed in 1666 after the Great Fire of London—work first started in 1862 and involved narrowing the River Thames with 22 acres of land. The quantities of materials give us some idea of the scale of these works: 650,000 cubic feet of granite, 80,000 cubic yards of brickwork, 140,000 cubic yards of concrete, 500,000 cubic feet of timber. Technical and technological innovations fueled the construction. The Victoria Embankment was the first roadway to be constantly lit by electricity, in 1878. While the aboveground surface was enriched with gardens, statues, and monuments, London's frenetic life moved underground, and for the first time the subterranean was seen as a complementary part of city life. Most important, the ultimate goal of these interventions was not merely hygienic— to remove muddy pockets from the city center. Rather, the embankment and similar projects represented the continuation belowground of a manifest strategy: to transform London into a global capital (fig. 1.01).

Two centuries later, at the 2014 Architecture Biennale in Venice, Rem Koolhaas / OMA explored the impact that inventions such as the elevator have had on architecture.[1] In the exhibition catalog *Elements of Architecture*, the Dutch architect compared the rising height of skyscrapers over the past 150 years with their negative—impressive excavations downward. This research showed that the deepest existing mines—2.5 miles deep—are at least four times deeper than the current highest skyscraper—the 3,281-foot-high Kingdom Tower in Jeddah. Both mines and skyscrapers require similar technological devices: elevators, ventilation systems, telephones, electricity, and so on.

That's why, in his book *Vertical*, Stephen Graham writes that skyscrapers can be read as inverted minescapes.[2] The construction of a tower requires tons of steel, concrete, glass, and aluminum. This implies the mining and exploitation of limestone, bauxite, coal, and other minerals. In other words, skyscrapers and mines are linked by the same production methods, and those methods are sometimes controversial and corrupt. Whereas digging and carving have long transformed the earth into a favorable environment for humans, the Industrial Revolution made the Underworld an ideal territory for exploiting the earth and human labor for profit. Today, mining is on the wane in Western countries but is still a fundamental asset in emerging economies such as South Africa, Colombia, and Bolivia. In fact, South Africa has two of the world's deepest mines.

Mponeng, the deepest gold mine in the world at 2.5 miles belowground, is southwest of Johannesburg on the border between the Gauteng and North West Provinces and is a perfect example of how gold exploitation is still a form of neocolonialism. The mine, originally known as Western Deep Levels South Shaft or No. 1 Shaft, opened in 1981. Its name was changed to Mponeng in 1999, and the mine is now undergoing an expansion that will

Fig. 1.01. Cross section through the Victoria Embankment, London. *Illustrated London News*, 1867.

extend its life until 2040. The mine currently produces 315,000 ounces of gold per year, which translates to approximately $400 million in gross revenues. The Witwatersrand basin has extremely hard rock, and the mining technology hasn't changed much over the years, but its invasive presence makes Mponeng a type of articulated underground city. Every day 4,000 workers descend the mine through a twin-shaft system that holds up to 120 people at a time: the main shaft takes workers up to 1.2 miles underground. From there a secondary shaft takes them farther underground, since a single vertical shaft can go only 1.2 miles deep. The deepest section of the mine is accessible only by vehicle or foot, and it is more than an hour from the surface. Furthermore, the temperature of the virgin rock reaches 151°F, so it is necessary to have an ice-making plant on the surface. Slurry ice is pumped down into the tunnels to maintain an acceptable temperature below 86°F. Ventilation is another issue that's partly addressed by enormous fans above vertical shafts. Excavated areas consist of stopes, or open spaces, and support columns to keep the openings stable. Then, cavities that have been mined are backfilled with concrete.

Technology is also used at the entrance to stop ghost miners, armed workers who try to steal gold. In Mponeng, every employee is tracked with facial-recognition technology. The incredible machinery deployed here transforms this mine into an invisible extension of modern city life with its own rituals and appetites (fig. 1.02).

Whereas the Mponeng Gold Mine is at the peak of its life cycle, Poland offers a different example of mining infrastructure,

Fig. 1.02. Mponeng Gold Mine, South Africa. *Courtesy of AngloGold Ashanti; photo: Chris Wessels*

one that has been converted to other uses in recent years and expresses the religious and social values of an entire community. The Wieliczka Salt Mine in the south is 178 miles long and reaches a depth of 1,072 feet on nine levels. It is an interesting example of spontaneous adaptive reuse, but also a symbol of the dynamic relationships among humans, technology, industry, and the underground.

Founded in the Middle Ages, this mine began producing table salt in the thirteenth century. Operations were interrupted during World War II, when the Nazis took over the shafts and installed an armament factory, bringing Jewish laborers from nearby concentration camps. After the war, operations resumed until the early 1990s, when the Wieliczka Salt Mine was turned into a tourist attraction. Visitors come to view the decorative work the miners left behind, such as wall carvings, furniture, and statues. Four chapels were built in addition to the Kinga Chapel, erected at the beginning of the twentieth century. The mine has an underground lake and a wellness center that attracts people suffering from respiratory illnesses. Since 1978 the Wieliczka Salt Mine has been on the UNESCO World Heritage List, not only because it shows

how mining techniques have evolved over the centuries, but for its historical and cultural significance (fig. 1.03).

Fig. 1.03. Aboveground and belowground view of Wieliczka Salt Mine, Poland (collage). Willem Hondius, 1598–1652. *Courtesy of Kpalion*

THE QUEST FOR WATER

If mines are the most ingenious manifestation of our desire to reach the unknown, the Underworld is also associated with something more utilitarian: civil engineering. By using the subterranean world as an infrastructural network, the early Romans introduced the idea of a direct correspondence between up and down, light and darkness. In Naples in southern Italy, the relationship between the city aboveground and its invisible counterpart has always been porous.[3]

Fig. 1.04. Piscina Mirabilis, Italy: longitudinal nave. *Courtesy of Stefano Corbo*

Although their first excavations date to 5,000 years ago, it was the Greeks, in the fourth century BCE, who opened tuff quarries here to build defensive walls and temples for the city they had founded—Neapolis. They also used the city underground to build funerary hypogea—niches for cremated or buried remains.

Later the Romans adopted this approach to create a capillary of tunnels, cisterns, and aqueducts. Today, Naples's underground is also populated by a rich accumulation of archeological remains that allow us to reconstruct the city's complex and stratified history. Just 130 feet beneath the surface one can find theaters, streets, catacombs, and markets. Invisible to most of its citizens, this 250-mile underground universe—an extended quarry—served the life of the aboveground city for more than 2,500 years by allowing today's Naples to be literally built from excavated volcanic tuff rock. This is why Naples is called the porous city—the underground has been gradually emptied.

Just a few kilometers from the city center, in the town of Bacoli, is another magnificent underground structure built in Roman times—the famous Piscina Mirabilis, one of the world's largest potable-water cisterns. It was built during the Augustan age between the end of the first century BCE and the beginning of the first century CE, mainly for military purposes. Given the unstable political climate, the imperial navy fleet, Classis Praetoria Misenensis Pia Vindex, was stationed in Miseno, a port facing the Gulf of Naples, and the cistern supplied water to the navy fleet and nearby villas. It collected water coming from the main Roman aqueduct, the Fontis Augustei Aquaeductum, 62 miles away from Naples. In this case, too, the cistern was dug into the tuff rock. At 236 feet long, 50 feet high, and 82 feet wide, its monumental size is emphasized by vaulted ceilings and fifty pillars. Five longitudinal naves and thirteen transversal naves articulate the interior spaces, which receive natural light at strategic points. The repetition of vaults and pillars changes the perception of a cistern, by giving the impression that it goes on endlessly. The tuff rock was originally covered with a waterproof layer, *opus signinum*, composed of broken tiles and mortar. The central nave was built about 3 feet lower than the rest of the space to allow for maintenance and emptying. Water was extracted through openings in the ceilings and distributed through secondary channels (fig. 1.04).

Similar to Piscina Mirabilis in Italy, the Basilica Cistern was the largest of hundreds of cisterns built beneath Istanbul over the centuries. Measuring 453 feet long and 213 feet wide, it was built in 532 CE by the Byzantine emperor Justinian I, on the former site of a Roman basilica originally erected between the third and fourth centuries BCE. The interior is based on a column grid of twelve by twenty-eight rows. The ceiling is supported by 336 marble columns whose capitals—mainly Ionic and Corinthian—were plundered from other sites. Around 7,000 slaves built the cistern, which supplied water to major buildings such as the Great Palace of Constantinople and, during the Ottomans, the Topkapi Palace. It could store up to 80,000 cubic meters—17.5 millions gallons—of water.

Gradually the Basilica Cistern fell into disuse, and it was only in the sixteenth century that Dutch traveler Petrus Gyllius, in Istanbul to research Byzantine ruins, managed to descend the steps that separated the cistern from the city and found this underground structure. The Basilica Cistern was restored in phases, primarily in the eighteenth and nineteenth centuries (fig. 1.05).

Fig. 1.05. Basilica Cistern, Turkey: interior view. *Courtesy of Dpnuevo*

Fig. 1.06. Chand Baori, India: detail of the stepwell structure

Water is the protagonist of another historical example of urban infrastructure that marries utilitarian purposes with religious and social needs. In India, the famous stepwells were ponds designed to store and supply water in times of drought. However, the water itself and the ritual of descending mysteriously into the earth transformed these structures into something else. The pursuit of leisure, in fact, was a significant aspect of the design of these stepwells. People used them to find relief from the heat, and their sunken surfaces were integrated into a subterranean system of galleries that offered protection from hot summers.

Ceremonies took place in the stepwells too, transforming them into a fundamental space for the community's social life. An example is Chand Baori, one of the largest stepwells built in the tenth century in Abhaneri, Rajasthan region, where the proximity to the Thar desert makes water supply a serious problem; summer temperatures hover around 100°F. Chand Baori is just one of the 3,000 stepwells built over the centuries in the region. At 100 feet deep, with 3,500 steps and thirteen levels, it is combined with a temple dedicated to Harshat Mata, the goddess of joy and happiness. Water has a symbolic meaning in Hindu mythology, serving as an intermediary between Earth and heaven. Separating the structure's spiritual and social components is impossible: Chand Baori not only provided water but became a place for prayer and meditation (fig. 1.06).

SURVEILLANCE AND CONTROL

When talking about secret spaces and urban infrastructure, we cannot forget about a building type whose formal articulation has been subject to many different interpretations: the prison. In East Granby, Connecticut, the melding of a mine and a prison produced the notorious Old Newgate, also known as the Hell—a peculiar example of underground conversion. At the beginning of the eighteenth century, copper was discovered in the region and a system of tunnels were dug for its extraction. Ore from the mine was shipped to Boston and then to England to be refined. In 1773 the Connecticut General Assembly transformed the tunnels into a prison and employed its inmates as miners. A 15-by-12-foot underground room was also excavated, and the prisoners were forced to live and work in those conditions. Only later, in 1790, were prison facilities added aboveground. Around 1850, the tunnels began attracting curious visitors, who toured the prison with candles. In 1968 the state bought the site, restored some of the original spaces, and built a tunnel for tourist access to the mines. Today the complex is a museum, part of the Old New-Gate Prison and Copper Mine Archaeological Reserve (fig. 1.07).

Prisons belong to the Underworld, especially if their design is inspired by the Panopticon principle, a social experiment conceived by Jeremy Bentham in 1791. The physical translation of his ideas, aimed to rethink the relationship between power and individuals, found its most successful expression in the prison. The Panopticon prison was a cylindrical building composed of various rings and generally topped by a dome. In the middle was a single, all-seeing Eye, a tower representing the invasive presence of Power, which sees everything without ever being seen. Every ring of the prison was characterized by individual cells with two windows: an exterior window that let daylight in, and an interior window so the Power could monitor the prisoners' behavior. The Panopticon principle introduced the notion of constant observation and surveillance. The inmates were alone; any collective desire for socialization was denied.

The most-famous examples of these prisons are Arnhem and Breda in the Netherlands, both designed by Johan Frederik

Fig. 1-07. Old Newgate Prison: ruins of the original brick structure

Fig. 1.08. Koepel Gevangenis, Breda. *Courtesy of Rijksdienst voor het Cultureel Erfgoed*

Metzelaar. Several proposals were offered for reuse of the Arnhem prison—in 1980–81, Rem Koolhaas proposed dismantling the original configuration and creating new spaces for collective use—but the Breda Panopticon, built between 1882 and 1886, continued operating as the Koepel Gevangenis prison until 2013 and was nominated as a national monument in 2001 (fig. 1.08).

Another more mysterious example is Torrione of Niccolò V, a tower and underground vault built by Bernardo Rossellino between 1451 and 1455 in Vatican City. Originally a prison inside the Leonine Walls, today it is the headquarters of a venerable bank: the Istituto per le Opere di Religione (IOR). Here the relationship between form and function is striking. The site that the Vatican authorities chose for their bank is somehow symbolic of the suspicious role it has played over the years in terms of money laundering, occult funding, and mysterious geopolitical affairs. Originally a local bank

Fig. 1.09. IOR Bank, Torrione di Niccolò V, Vatican City: aerial view

for Vatican citizens, IOR later became an offshore entity. From the outside, it looks like an inexpugnable bunker. Its 30-foot-thick walls protect its secrets from any process of transparency that similar banks are subject to around the world. For many years, mystery has haunted IOR's activities; it was rumored to have 130 employees and about 44,000 saving accounts. Customers were identified through a code number only, and operations were not trackable. Its business was known only to the pope and a few other Vatican authorities. In 2012, for the first time in its history, IOR opened its doors to journalists. In 2013 the bank published its financial holdings and has since adopted a more transparent way of doing business (fig. 1.09).

TRANSIT SYSTEMS

Building underground continues today, of course. The need to reduce traffic congestion in cities has led to the construction of highway tunnels, subway lines, and transportation hubs. Montreal's Underground City (RÉSO), for instance, is a subterranean series of hotels, shops, offices, residences, and entertainment venues integrated with the city's rapid-transit system, allowing citizens to enjoy city life protected from the severe winters. Development of this underground network began in the 1960s with a shopping center, Place Villa-Marie, designed by urbanist Vincent Ponte, who envisioned a new urban model that separated cars and pedestrians—a solution to the continuing out-migration from cities to escape the traffic.

Inspired by Leonardo da Vinci's sixteenth-century urban projects, Ponte designed a multilayered environment where cars are left on the surface, pedestrians are directed belowground, and public transportation is one more level down. If Place Villa-Marie (1962) was just the beginning of this experiment—the first of RÉSO's multiple nodes—the Olympic Games that Montreal hosted in 1967 were a catalyst for completing the subway system and building a series of complementary facilities around the stations. RÉSO's success, in fact, depended on its flexibility and capacity to grow. Over time, RÉSO has evolved more as an indoor city than as an underground city, since most of its nodes are at ground level. Today the network is composed of 120 access points, sixty residential complexes, seven metro stations, and two commuter train stations. RÉSO also includes hotels, museums, and universities, and more than 500,000 people pass through every day (fig. 1.10).

Fig. 1.10. Montreal underground network (RÉSO): Complexe Desjardins. *Courtesy of Guilhem Vellut*

Fig. 1.11. Canary Wharf Metro Station, London: view from escalator. *Courtesy of Mattbuck*

Today, metro stations are the most-common urban examples of the design possibilities for the Underworld. In London, Canary Wharf station, designed in 1999 by Norman Foster and Partners, was part of the Jubilee Line, eleven stations connecting North and South London diagonally. Built 88 feet below the city on the footprint of the former West India Dock, the station is 820 feet long and 100 feet wide, a longitudinal atrium. Shops, kiosks, and offices sit along the perimeter over four floors, so that the main space is completely open except for twenty blocks of escalators. Every day 100,000 commuters use this station. Outside, three organic canopies announce its presence (fig. 1.11).

Not all tunnels and subway systems were destined for such greatness. Many are now leftover spaces, abandoned structures that never functioned properly. That's what happened in Bratislava, Slovakia. Communist authorities built the Bratislava metro in 1974 as a transportation link between the city center and one of its densest districts: Petržalka, a complex of social housing consisting of high-rise prefabricated concrete buildings. With fewer than a million residents, it could not call the underground system a subway, so the official name was fast train. Unfortunately, the city never benefited from these fast trains, since the first phase wasn't due for completion until 1997. The Communist regime collapsed and construction stopped for good in 1990 (fig. 1.12).

The Cincinnati subway suffered a similar fate. Now the largest abandoned tunnel system in the US, the 16-mile underground loop was meant to relieve traffic congestion. Historically, electric cars began to populate the city in 1888 and soon became the main form of transportation. By the turn of the twentieth century, Cincinnati, with its growing economy, was one of the most populous cities in the US. Plans for a metro system got underway in 1916 but were scrapped in 1928 because of high construction costs and the onset of the Great Depression. Six miles of infrastructure and 2.2 miles of tunnels were built. Six stations were completed: three underground and three aboveground. While the underground stations are intact, the exterior stations were demolished. Several proposals were offered for repurposing the tunnels; in 2002 a regional rail system was discussed but not approved (fig. 1.13).

Even when underworld spaces become obsolete, however, they are often a source of stories and legends that tell us about local culture. The Cobble Hill Tunnel in Brooklyn, New York, also called Atlantic Avenue—an abandoned railway tunnel built in 1844—is one of the oldest railway structures in North America. Part of the Long Island Railroad that ran between New York City and Boston, Cobble Hill was 17 feet high, 21 feet wide, and 2,500 feet long. Despite its popularity, its life span was very short. In 1861 the New York state legislature banned locomotives from Brooklyn and the tunnel was sealed off. However, its invisible presence continued to mark city life: in 1916, German terrorists were suspected of using the tunnel to make bombs and plan an attack, but the police found nothing. A few years later, during Prohibition, Cobble Hill was rumored to be a whiskey warehouse. And in 1941, the FBI checked out a rumor that spies were hiding there, but again nothing was found. After years of neglect, the tunnel was temporary reopened as a tourist attraction in the 1980s and in 1989 was listed on the National Register of Historic Places (fig. 1.14).

Fig. 1.12. Bratislava Metro Line, Slovakia: ruins of the incomplete station. *Courtesy of Rafticek*

Fig. 1.13. Cincinnati subway, Race St. Station. *Courtesy of Jonathan Warren*

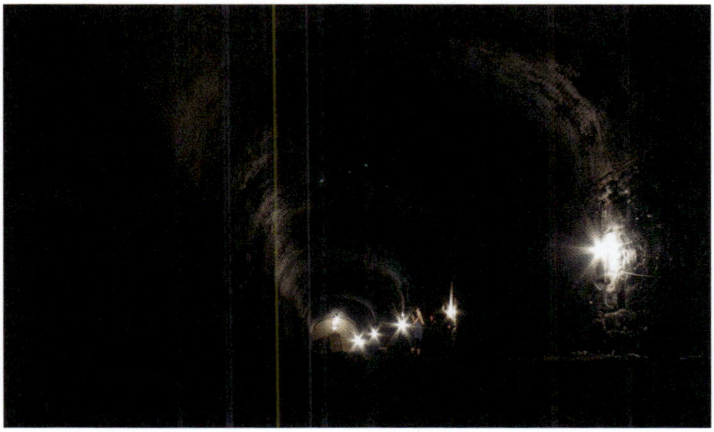

Fig. 1.14. Cobble Hill Tunnel, Brooklyn: interior view. *Courtesy of Matt Baume*

DATA CENTERS: THE RISE OF A NEW TYPOLOGY

A study of modern cities through the lens of the Underworld would be incomplete without a look at data storage. Since the second half of the twentieth century, the need to store computer data and servers has been an increasingly pressing issue. With the proliferation of the internet in the 1990s, a new and more urgent kind of facility was born: the data center, highly advanced technological warehouses that ensure fast connectivity, security, and nonstop operation. Data centers are similar to industrial complexes and demand a huge amount of electricity to function. Their presence is normally isolated from the city center and protected from any possible interference. Since the internet can also be a target of espionage or cyberwar—an extension of the Cold War in the twenty-first century—the design of data centers has military and political implications. However, the information we have about these structures is mainly limited to centers run by internet service providers whose main goal is to store their own servers and not to safeguard sensitive data.

The Alcalá Data Center, a few kilometers outside Madrid, is one of the biggest data-processing centers in the world. Built by Telefónica—the Spanish broadband and telecommunication provider serving primarily Central and South America—the design program called for, among other things, a research lab and an innovation center providing public guided tours. The first phase, completed in 2013, consisted of seven of the planned twenty-three IT rooms. Its super-energy-efficient construction was based on repeating, modular units for easy and relatively low-cost expansion. Each of the IT rooms—around 7,330 square feet each—can work independently of the others and service customers in the UK, Germany, and other European countries. More than a hundred commercial customers use this center. Inside, the temperature is kept at 64–75°F. Conditioned air is recycled using the latest technologies to keep the building cool despite the heat generated by the equipment. With the first phase completed, fifty workers occupy the Alcalá Data Center. Its activity can also be monitored remotely (fig. 1.15).

The symbolic *fil rouge* or common thread between the military world and data protection is on display at Pionen White Mountain, a former nuclear bunker in Stockholm, 100 feet below Vita Berg Park, which was originally built in 1943 to protect government activities from enemy attacks. In 2008, the bunker was transformed

Fig. 1.15. Telefónica Data Center, Alcalá de Henares, Spain

into a data center by architect Albert France-Lanord. Light, plants, water, and technology are imported from the exterior world to create a pleasantly habitable environment that includes waterfalls, daylight, and even greenhouses. You might say that inanimate rock has been transformed into a living organism occupied by humans and other living beings. Home to the Wikileaks server, among others, Pionen White Mountain is still a bunker, an impassable fortress, in contrast to the transparency and free access implicit in information technology. Sealed behind a 16-inch-thick door, the outside world is considered a potential source of danger. Although White Mountain is one of the first projects to deeply question the design and role of data centers in society—no doubt inspiring further developments—its inaccessibility exemplifies the contradictions and ambiguities that come with new building types (fig. 1.16).

On the island of Spitsbergen in Norway, 800 miles from the North Pole, is the Svalbard Global Seed Vault, the biggest

repository of agricultural biodiversity in the world. A hybrid structure—part seed bank, part bunker, part data center—it was funded by the Norwegian government and opened its doors in 2008. The government owns the building but not its content, which is why different countries, from the United States to North Korea, agreed to deposit copies of their plant seeds in Svalbard. Its purpose is twofold: to preserve genetic diversity and protect seeds from natural disasters or other accidents.

Fig. 1.16. Pionen / White Mountain Data Center, Stockholm: natural or artificial? *Courtesy of Albert France-Lanord Architects; photo: Åke E:son Lindman*

Compared to the other 1,700-some seed banks around the world, Svalbard Global Seed Vault is said to provide optimal conditions and tight security. The location was considered ideal because Spitsbergen is roughly 430 feet above sea level—high enough to protect the vault from rising waters when the ice melts. Built by Peter W. Søderman MNAL of Barlindhaug Consult, the vault resembles a ship that has wrecked in an ice-filled sea. On the exposed part of the facade is a series of mirrors and prisms by artist Dyveke Sanne. Inside, a 390-foot-long tunnel goes straight into the permafrost, where three underground rooms store the seeds at a temperature of −0.4°F, which will significantly delay aging. By 2017, the vault was storing more than 930,000 examples of seeds, but it has the capacity to store up to 4.5 million crop varieties—each variety containing an average of 500 seeds. The vault's location and construction underscore the Underworld's importance as a place of protection and refuge. Yet, despite all this, in 2017 it flooded due to unusually high temperatures. The Norwegian government is investing $4.4 million to upgrade the structure and safeguard it from such risks in the future (fig. 1.17).

Fig. 1.17. Svalbard Global Seed Vault, Norway: the only visible part of the structure

TWO

DESIGN AS WARFARE

As French philosopher Henri Lefebvre wrote in *The Production of Space*[1], space is never neutral; it controls our bodies and actions and tell us what direction to take. Space has orientations, means, and filters, because it's always the product of specific political and economic decisions. When we look into our cities, these conditions clearly express the relationship between Power and its citizens. In other words, the city appears to be a place of conflict between individuals and societal order, regulated by cultural, religious, and juridical institutions.

As seen in the previous chapter, the Underworld offers the ideal environment for maintaining control and vigilance. The devastating effects of World War II caused many countries to use it as a hidden defense system. Most of these military structures are invisible to our eyes, and maps and plans offer a superficial picture. Warfare can be understood only in its three-dimensional character, depicting both a visible battlefield and an invisible world characterized by a network of underground tunnels. The Soviet Union and the United States provide the best examples of infrastructure built to protect the population and heads of state.

THE EASTERN BLOC

When it comes to invisible networks, it's impossible not to start with Moscow's underground, which has a long history of mysterious engineering projects. The first tunnels were probably built in the fourteenth century underneath the Kremlin by Prince Dmitry Donskoy and were meant to serve as escape routes. Ivan the Terrible (1530–1584) used the underground to store his arsenal, and historians theorize that a subterranean library consisting of gold-covered books was built in Moscow during the sixteenth century.

The Neglinnaya, a 4.6-mile-long underground river that once crossed Moscow from north to south, is also part of its secret history. By the mid-eighteenth century, the river became a contaminated sewer thanks to the growing population and industrial expansion. In 1792 it was diverted into a new canal and the riverbed was filled. After a great fire in 1812, the Neglinnaya was covered with a vault and buried underground. Although the river runs too deep to be visible today, its echo still resounds (fig. 2.01).

Another project, Moscow Metro-2, was a secret underground metro system whose planning started under Stalin's regime in response to the missile sites and bunkers the United States constructed in the 1960s. Shrouded in mystery, since the Russian Ministry of Defense never confirmed or denied it, Metro-2 was said to be composed of four lines 165 feet deep that connected the major governmental buildings: the Kremlin, the KGB headquarters, and the airport. The network also included shelters for the Communist leadership. Writer Vladimir Gonik stated that each member of the Central Committee was assigned an underground, 1,935-square-foot apartment equipped with a lounge, studio, kitchen, and bathroom.

One of the stops on Metro-2 was the famous city of Ramenki, a bunker southwest of Moscow near Moscow State University. Built about 60 feet beneath the city, this bunker could accommodate up to 15,000 people. Sources say it was built in the 1960s and 1970s and could shelter people for thirty years in case of nuclear attack (fig. 2.02).

Fig. 2.01. Apollinary Vasnetsov. *The Old Mouth of the River Neglinnaya*, 1924.

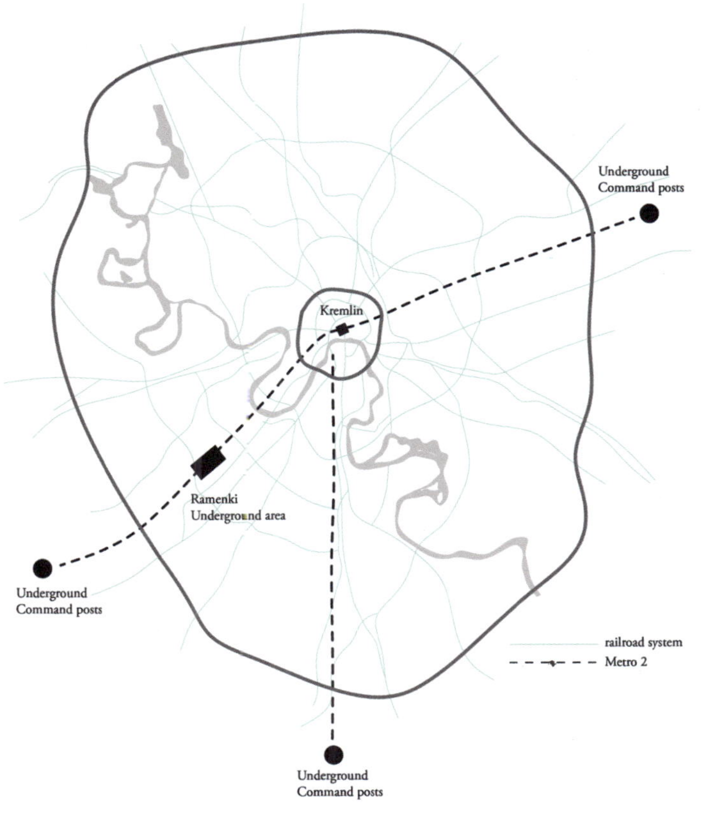

Fig. 2.02. Hypothetical map of Moscow Metro-2, according to US Military intelligence. *Illustration by Stefano Corbo, 2018*

Fig. 2.03. Pyongyang Metro, North Korea: Puhung Station

Another Communist country—North Korea—constructed a similar underground system that could shelter civilians. Construction on Pyongyang's subway began in 1965; it was designed to transport between 300,000 and 700,000 people and also house political and military authorities in case of attack. At 328 feet belowground, it is the deepest subway in the world and consists of two lines and sixteen stations. The station names relate to aspects of North Korea's revolution rather than their location stops.

China supplied the equipment, and its trains were recycled from East Germany. The stations are literally holes in the ground, invisible on the street. And like Moscow's metro, Pyongyang stations are furnished with statues and mosaics that celebrate North Korea's history and, above all, President Kim Il-Sung. The result is a massive form of propaganda. Before 2010, only two stations were open to foreign visitors. Later, six stations were opened, and now the entire network is accessible (fig. 2.03).

Although the two countries belonged to the same Communist bloc, the deteriorating relationship between China and the Soviet Union led Mao Zedong to order China's own subterranean city, Dixia Cheng, between 1969 and 1979 to protect the population from possible nuclear attack. More than 300,000 civilians collaborated with Beijing authorities on its design, and its size could be compared to another famous Chinese landmark: the Great Wall. In the absence of reliable information, one has to defer to the Chinese government, which stated that at the time of its official conclusion, Dixia Cheng could eventually host the entire population of the city center—around six million in 1969. A functional city, and not just a dispersed series of tunnels and rooms, Dixia Cheng had more than ninety entrances spread over the center of Beijing, and a diverse program of activities: 10,000 shelters, plus schools, theaters, shops, restaurants, a roller-skating rink, and other sport facilities. Complex ventilation systems were installed, with more than 2,000 shafts able to be closed off in case of gas attacks.

Another Dixia Cheng is rumored to exist, made of secret passageways connecting the most-important governmental buildings. Some also hypothesize that the city's major monuments were linked to each other. Fortunately, Dixia Cheng was never used as a bomb shelter, and over the decades it has been progressively privatized and adapted to other uses. During the mass migration of farmers to the city that began in the late 1980s, some of Dixia Cheng's tunnels were turned into low-cost housing. In 2010, Beijing authorities prohibited their residential use but allowed the creation of ten community centers equipped with libraries, reading rooms, and cafés. Dixia Cheng has been closed for renovation since 2008 (fig. 2.04).

Another model for reconverting bomb shelters comes from Nanjing, where a former bunker, recently used for government parking, has been transformed into a temple to culture. Librairie Avant-Garde is a subterranean, 40,687-square-foot bookstore that opened just outside Nanjing University campus in 2004. Visitors descend to the entrance on a long ramp, where they encounter a checkout desk and lobby and a second ramp that takes them to the main hall. This is a true public space accommodating concerts, talks, and exhibitions, plus areas for workshops and retail. The main hall's library—two long rows of tables and more than 300 seats—allows visitors to stop, sit, and read (fig. 2.05).

Fig. 2.04. Dixia Cheng, Beijing: one of ninety entrances to the underground city

Fig. 2.05. Avant-Garde Bookstore, Nanjing: a temple dedicated to culture. *Courtesy of Joseph Lai*

THE UNITED STATES, ASIA, AND THE MIDDLE EAST

During the Cold War, the American Strategic Air Command built hundreds of missile silos in remote rural areas. From these spots, missiles could be launched to the other side of the world. In a few cases, the dismantled missile silos have been given a new life. One example is the Air Force Facility Missile Site 8 in Sahuarita, Arizona, the only remaining Titan II intercontinental ballistic missile (ICBM) complex out of the fifty that existed between 1963 and 1987. Titan II missiles were designed to resist a Soviet nuclear attack and to counterattack; they could be launched in less than a minute. The silo was integrated with a three-story cylindrical Launch Control Center isolated by heavy blast doors. Two cables connected the center to the missile silo, which was theoretically isolated from radiation and nerve agents through a 740-ton door.

In 1981 the Titan II ICBMs became obsolete and were destroyed, but the facility was turned into the Titan Missile Museum in 1986 and a lone survivor was put on display. Visitors can enter the silo and tour a series of spaces that were originally part of this military complex. What was once a strategic military space has become a national landmark (fig. 2.06).

In Abilene, Texas, an underground missile silo was converted to a private residence. In 1997, Bruce Townsley paid $99,000 for the silo and some of the employee living quarters. Two years later

Fig. 2.06. Titan Missile Museum, Sahuarita, Arizona: view of the missile from the underground silo. *Courtesy of Patrick Finnegan*

Fig. 2.07. Missile silo house, Texas: the main living space. *Courtesy of Bruce Townsley*

he moved into the renovated 2,200-square-foot house. Entering is a long process of descent on a narrow staircase. The main living space is a concrete ring with a large column in the middle: white partitions separate the kitchen, office, bedroom, and other rooms in a radial floor plan. The lower-level plan, containing a bathroom and gym, is identical to the upper floor plan. A tunnel connects the house to the 185-foot silo—an empty Cold War memento (fig. 2.07).

Indeed, the reuse of defunct belowground governmental structures often depends on the initiative of private interests. The Dupont Underground, in one of the busiest districts in Washington, DC, is an example of a neglected space being used as a wartime bunker and eventually given back to the city to support theater, music, and art. In 1949, a trolley station was built 10 feet below the street, and in 1962 it was turned into an atomic-bomb shelter. In 1974, after squatters claimed it, the city sealed the nine station entrances. In its latest iteration, architect Julian Hunt has converted this cavernous space into a 75,000-square-foot platform for art and musical performances. With its 20-foot-wide concrete tunnels and remnant trolley tracks, the first phase will provide 14,000 square feet for dance performances. Dupont Underground

Fig. 2.08. Dupont Underground, Washington, DC: tunnels are transformed into an art gallery. *Courtesy of Daniel Lobo*

aims to act as a spontaneous countermodel of the famous Smithsonian Museum by investing in young, unknown artists[2] (fig. 2.08).

In the 1960s, if the Soviet Union was a constant yet silent enemy, a more traditional war was playing out in Vietnam. The Viet Cong launched guerrilla warfare with a capillary network of tunnels devised to throw the Americans off guard. The Cu Chi tunnels beneath the Cu Chi district in Saigon were actually dug in the 1940s during the war against the French colonial army. But when the United States increased its presence in Vietnam, the tunnels were reactivated. Their entrances camouflaged and booby-trapped, they served as hiding places during combat and as transport for weapons, food, and messengers. The tunnels even housed hospitals and other structures for soldiers, such as theaters and music halls.

However, living conditions in the Cu Chi tunnels were terrible. The tunnels were infested with scorpions, ants, and other animals, and air and water were scarce. Malaria spread rapidly and many people died. Nevertheless, this underground network was used for a long time to resist the American offensive. Viet Cong soldiers could wait out massive bombing operations below the ground, and it was very difficult for American soldiers to detect and destroy these structures. In 1967, when the Americans finally raided the Viet Cong headquarters of Cu Chi, they found documents containing Viet Cong strategy and maps of US bases. Vietnamese authorities estimate that 45,000 men and women lost their lives defending the Cu Chi tunnels, which have been preserved as public memorial parks (fig. 2.09).

Fig. 2.09. Cu Chi tunnels, Vietnam: camouflage and the art of war. *Courtesy of Thomas Schoch*

Fig. 2.10. Rafah: Israel Defense Forces find a tunnel with concrete walls hidden by a civilian home. *Courtesy of Israel Defense Forces*

Similar dynamics are at work in the Gaza Strip, where, over the last ten years, the Arab-Israeli conflict has moved underground. In the 1970s, the governing authority funded construction of hundreds of tunnels to move weapons, people, food, and other goods into the Palestinian territory.[3] The construction quality is slightly better than Vietnam's tunnels, since they are made of concrete and wired for electricity. According to analysts, the Gaza tunnels serve three functions: they are defensive, used as a command center and arsenal; they are offensive, used for attacks on the Israeli border; and they are a link to Egypt.

Whereas Palestinians are supposed to control a portion of territory on the basis of the Oslo Accords (1993), Israel controls the airspace, water aquifers, and underground. In 2014 the Israeli army began demolishing the tunnels. Sensors and transmitters have been deployed to detect these invisible structures, and so far, thirty-two have been destroyed with explosives, according to Israeli numbers (fig. 2.10).

WESTERN EUROPE

The ghost of the Cold War also haunted the core of Europe. Bunkers and tunnels permeated some of Sweden's most urbanized areas starting in the late 1930s, though construction was often complicated due to Stockholm's granite bedrock. Between

1952 and 1957, a shelter for 20,000 people was built in Södermalm, under the Katarina Mountain. In the mid-1960s, a new bunker in Norrmalm expanded the underground network. More than 65,000 shelters have been counted in Sweden.

Lucerne, Switzerland, is home to one of the largest civilian bunkers. Built between 1970 and 1976, the Sonnenberg tunnel could accommodate around 20,000 people in case of war. It consisted of two motorway tunnels—one running in each direction and each capable of housing 10,000 people—and a seven-story underground building containing a hospital, radio studio, ventilation equipment, prison, and other facilities. The two tunnels could be isolated with four doors that were 5 feet thick and weighed 350 tons.

The structure was the result of a 1963 federal law requiring that fallout shelters be provided for the entire Swiss population. Many small bunkers were built, since every citizen had the right to construct a personal shelter. The Sonnenberg tunnel was never used for its intended purpose, but testing uncovered some problems: closing it off took longer than expected—almost an entire day—as did setting up 20,000 beds. After long debate, in 2006 authorities approved a redesign of the complex. The central seven-story building was converted to a shelter able to accommodate 2,000 people, and the remaining spaces were preserved as a tourist attraction—a frustrated monument to the Cold War (fig. 2.11).

Finland, too, mandated the construction of shelters to protect its citizens from nuclear attack. One is on the outskirts of Helsinki, surrounded by a natural reserve. Quarried from granite between

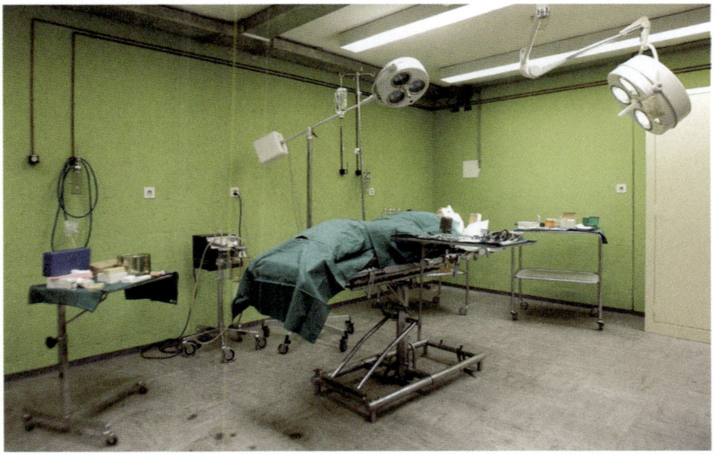

Fig. 2.11. Sonnenberg bunker, Switzerland: reconstruction of the original hospital's operation room. *Courtesy of Andrea Huwyler-Bachmann*

Fig. 2.12. Itäkeskus swimming complex, Helsinki: view of the main pool. *Courtesy of HKP Architects, Helsinki; photo: Jussi Tiainen*

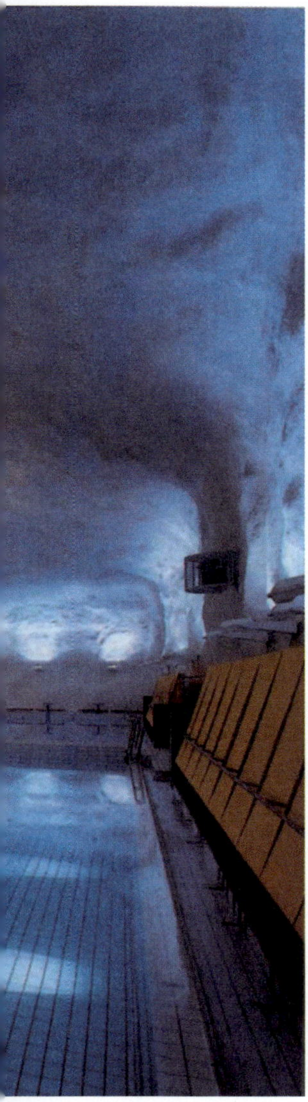

1989 and 1993 and able to accommodate around 3,500 people, Itäkeskus sits 105 feet below ground and, oddly, includes a series of swimming pools. A glazed pavilion marks the main entrance to the two-story structure. The first level houses an information desk, gym, and café. Below are the swimming pools and living spaces. Roughly 10,760 square feet, the complex includes whirlpool baths, saunas, Turkish baths, solaria, and other facilities. Knowing these amenities were available apparently helped ease the public's anxieties about the threat of nuclear war. And having a bunker that also functioned as a sports facility made the project cost-effective (fig. 2.12).

Another example of how the reuse of underground military structures can offer interesting design challenges comes from Berlin, where the London-based architect John Pawson converted two bunkers into a private museum: the Feuerle Collection. Connected at basement level, the bunkers—with 11-foot ceilings, 5-foot-thick columns, and 6.5-foot-thick concrete walls—were originally designed to protect the telecommunication system during World War II. Rather than changing their monumental aspect, Pawson worked by contrast, defining the spaces with ephemeral materials: sound, silence, incense, and water. The 70,000-square-foot bunkers are organized around several exhibition spaces. The ground floor contains temporary exhibitions, offices, and a reception area, while the basement contains themed exhibitions: the Lake Room, the Sound Room, and the Incense Room—homage to a spiritual tradition more than 2,000 years old. The Incense Room is furnished with a ceremonial table designed by Pawson himself.

The museum exhibits seventh-to-thirteenth-century Asian sculptures, Chinese Imperial furniture, and work by contemporary artists, including Anish Kapoor and James Lee Byars. Pawson turned intermittent flooding from an adjacent canal into an opportunity by creating the Lake Room behind a glass wall. The water heats the entire museum via a geothermal pump. The roof, with its large vents, was preserved and the interior concrete surfaces were cleaned and left exposed.

Pawson's intervention honors the concept of the bunkers by highlighting the role of the senses in such spaces. His minimal gestures allow a silent landscape to emerge from the repetitive concrete columns; visitors can concentrate on the artwork and appreciate the unique character of each exhibit area (fig. 2.13).

In the Netherlands in 2010, RAAF Studio and Atelier de Lyon redesigned one of 700 concrete bunkers composing the famous

Fig. 2.13. Désiré Feuerle Collection, Berlin: outside view of the Incense Room. *Female Divinity*, Khmer, Baphuon, eleventh century, stone. Khmer sculptures reflections. *Courtesy: def image © The Feuerle Collection*

NDW—New Dutch Waterline, a nineteenth-century military infrastructure that was active until 1940. Its goal was to secure Dutch cities such as Utrecht and Muiden. Presented with a small, house-like structure that could hold up to thirteen soldiers, the Bunker 599 redesign addressed two different aspects. One was the ambiguity between memory—its original meaning—and irony—the act of cutting the bunker in two, aiming to break down its massive character and finally make it accessible. The other was to establish a connection between the bunker, a nearby flooded area, and an adjacent natural reserve.

Fig. 2.14. Bunker 599, Netherlands: reinventing icons. *Courtesy of Hielkje Zijlstra, 2012*

A public promenade cuts the military structure into two, revealing the empty interior. The bunker becomes a metaphysical sculpture without a specific function. Instead, this deconstructed building serves as a territorial landmark, an ironic reminder of war times. The wooden pathway emphasizes the iconic cut in the building and leads visitors to the flooded area, which was originally designed to be deliberately flooded in case of enemy attack. If Dupont Underground's project in Washington, DC, was meant to give an abandoned structure back to the city life, RAAF and Atelier de Lyon's work interprets the bunker as an archeological sediment absorbed into the landscape (fig. 2.14).

In 2014, B-ILD Architects converted another bunker in the New Dutch Waterline into a tiny weekend retreat. Measuring just 9 by 9 feet and 6 feet high, the Bunker Pavilion is an experiment in flexible, multiuse spaces. It functions as a bedroom and living room with different configurations, thanks to furniture that can be folded, opened, and even retracted into the wall. The entrance and kitchen are also inventive, in-between spaces. And a wooden deck-platform doubles the usable space, providing an alfresco dining area and panoramic views. Not only do the bunker and the deck have the same footprint, but the deck boards are the same size as the ones used to make the board-formed concrete bunker (fig. 2.15).

Fig. 2.15. Bunker Pavilion, Netherlands, B-ILD Architects. *Courtesy of B-ILD Architects; photo: Tim Van de Velde*

THREE

LIFE AND DEATH IN THE UNDER-WORLD

On November 9, 1964, an exhibition opened at the Museum of Modern Art in New York City called *Architecture Without Architects: An Introduction to Non-Pedigreed Architecture*. In the preface to the book accompanying the show, its curator, Bernard Rudofsky, wrote the following:

"Architectural history, as written and taught in the Western world, has never been concerned with more than a few selected cultures. In terms of space it comprises but a small part of the globe—Europe, stretches of Egypt, Anatolia—or little more than was known in the second century A.D.

. . . Besides, architectural history is equally biased on the social plane. It amounts to little more than a who's who of architects who commemorated power and wealth; an anthology of buildings of, by, and for the privileged—the houses of true and false gods, of merchant princes and princes of the blood—with never a word about the houses of lesser people.

. . . Architecture Without Architects attempts to break down our narrow concepts of the art of building by introducing the unfamiliar world of non-pedigreed architecture. It is so little known that we don't even have a name for it. For want of a generic label, we shall call it vernacular, anonymous, spontaneous, indigenous, rural, as the case may be."[1]

The exhibit featured communal architecture from India, China, Africa, and the Middle East—a result of the constant, silent, and informal labor of entire communities that over the centuries have built their own habitat. One area of focus was cave dwellings—housing examples that are unusual and yet common in many parts of the world.

Unbeknown to each other, these civilizations shaped their dwellings in similar ways that have produced clear housing types. Subterranean houses and villages are, in fact, found in the Mediterranean region, North Africa, and Asia. As we'll see in the following pages, geology and climate were the factors influencing design and resulted in various types of housing: underground dwellings, cliff dwellings, and an intermediate condition—sunken courtyards.

DOMESTICITY IN EARLY CIVILIZATIONS

Mesa Verde, a Colorado national park containing thousands of archeological sites, is an example of how humans have inhabited the Underworld since early times. The park includes 600 cliff dwellings built by the Ancestral Puebloans— an ancient Native American culture living mostly in Utah, New Mexico, Arizona, and Colorado beginning in the twelfth century. While they never developed a writing system, their history has been reconstructed thanks to the buildings they left behind. Researchers discovered that the Puebloans used the golden mean and other mathematical formulas to make their houses. What remains today is a diverse collection of dwellings, from one-room units to microvillages composed of hundreds of rooms. The Cliff Palace, for example, was a sequence of 150 rooms and twenty-three kivas—large, round underground structures used for gatherings and rituals—and had a population of one hundred people. The presence of so many kivas led to the theory that the Cliff Palace was a social and administrative site rather than a simple aggregation of dwellings. Rooms were 6 to 8 feet high, accessible from the roof with ladders, and colorfully plastered. Smaller rooms were used to store corn and beans. Puebloans occupied Mesa Verde for more than a century before migrating south because of climate change, population growth, and conflict (fig. 3.01).

Dwellings can be either a scattered constellation of units or clustered in microvillages. What we find in Cappadocia, the Central Anatolia region of Turkey, is unique. One of the largest settlements, Derinkuyu, is a multilayered city that accommodated up to 20,000 people at a depth of more than 250 feet. Its eighteen or so levels are connected by hallways and narrow staircases. Similar to what was seen in Naples, the soft, volcanic tuff favored this labyrinthine type of construction.

Derinkuyu's history is unclear due to the area's political instability, but Anatolia was occupied and conquered by many different groups. Some scholars believe that the Hittites built Derinkuyu before 1200 BCE. Other scholars believe that the Phrygians founded it between 1200 and 800 BCE and that later Persians, Macedonians, Greeks, and Syrians were present in the region. What is certain is that the city's form was crystalized during the Byzantine era, when many Greek Christians found refuge here from Muslim persecution.

Greeks kept expanding this underground network until the early 1900s when the Turks forced them to leave and the tunnels were abandoned (1923). In 1963, almost by chance, Derinkuyu's underground city was discovered and brought to light. The impressive network of tunnels, rooms, and caverns contained not only dwellings but also food storage rooms, oil and wine presses, weapon storage areas, public spaces, churches, tombs, and stables. Its design and structure expressed the community's self-sufficient character. All eighteen levels could be sealed off with gigantic circular stone doors that opened and closed only from inside. Secondary passages were narrow enough to force people to walk in single file, so that it would have been very hard for troops to penetrate this underground city. Escape routes have been found on each level.

In peacetime, the city was also used for cold storage and an underground barn. Ventilation and water were provided through more than fifty air shafts, some of which worked as wells. These wells were inaccessible from the exterior. In addition, an underground river supplied water through a capillary irrigation system. Derinkuyu is close to another equally impressive settlement named Kaymakli. Some archeologists hypothesize that these two cities were connected by a 5-mile-long tunnel (figs. 3.02 and 3.03).

Durinkuyu and Kaymakli are underground examples of domestication, whereas Göreme Valley dwellings are formed from vertical rocks shaped by wind and water. Located in the same region as those two cities—a plateau 3,300 feet above sea level—this volcanic landscape is characterized by the irregular repetition of cones, pinnacles, and mushrooms that over the centuries have served as shelters. Desire for solitude and ascetic life pushed some 30,000 anchorites to live here in a type of fragmented monastic community, especially during the seventh century. Rooms, chapels, and other spaces were carved out of these rocks, accessible only by ladder (fig. 3.04).

Fig. 3.01. Mesa Verde, Colorado: the Cliff Palace. *Photo: Gustaf Nordenskiöld, 1891*

SURGU KAPI
STONE

Similar to Cappadocia, the Sassi settlements in Matera, the Basilicata region of southern Italy, are one of the most intact examples of troglodyte settlements in the Mediterranean. The caves were in constant use from 7000 BCE until the second half of the twentieth century. Over time, churches, cisterns, gardens, fortifications, and underground water tanks were built. The Sassi cover an area of 1,000 hectares (ha) (2,510 acres) and are composed of two main neighborhoods separated by a Romanesque cathedral erected in the thirteenth century. This city's unusual morphological condition resulted from the action of the Gravina River, which gradually created a deep ravine into which the cave dwellings were carved. Houses were normally arranged around a south-facing courtyard so that the sun's lower angle warmed the houses in winter. Temperature was always a constant 58°F. Central courtyards, typically with a collective oven, were spaces for social life.

Fig. 3.02. Derinkuyu: one of the stone doors sealing off the city from enemies. *Courtesy of Nevit Dilmen*

Fig. 3.03. Kaymakli, Cappadocia: interior view. *Courtesy of Gaspar Ros*

Fig. 3.04. Göreme cones. *Photo: John Henry Haynes (1884 or 1887)*

Fig. 3.05. Sassi di Matera, Italy: urban density

People and animals lived together, and without running water or electricity the settlements had a high infant mortality rate and were plagued by malaria. In the 1980s, the caves were made into tourist attractions, and in 1993 Matera was named a UNESCO World Heritage site (fig. 3.05).

Pantalica, Anapo Valley, also in southern Italy, contains an interesting mix of dwellings, tombs, and sacred spaces. Sicels, an Italic tribe who occupied the island more than 3,000 years ago, carved a necropolis out of the limestone cliffs. In the Middle Age these burial grounds became dwellings. Apartments with more than two rooms were gradually formed by connecting the former caves with interior passageways. Medieval chapels are also present, enriched with traces of frescoes. Italian archeologist Paolo Orsi excavated the site in the late nineteenth century (fig. 3.06).

In Andalusia, southern Spain, more than 2,000 dwellings have been built below the ground since the late fifteenth century, when the Moriscos—Moors forced to become Christians after Granada Reconquista in 1492—fled from the major cities to erect their houses in this area, which was already inhabited in the Stone Age. Laid out on an east–west axis, Gaudix cave houses were modeled out of tuff rock and followed a structural logic. Interior walls were 5 to 7 feet thick, and the average room was about 10 feet wide. Vaulted ceilings balanced lateral loads. Only small, white chimneys and a white facade signaled their presence.

As we've seen in Matera, climate played a crucial role in their design. The caves' thermal qualities allowed them to maintain an

Fig. 3.06. Pantalica, Sicily: view of the tombs-dwellings. *Courtesy of Pietro Columba*

annual average temperature of 60–70°F, whether the outside temperature was 100°F in summertime or 30°F in winter. From the top of the hill, one notices a striking contrast between the chimneys' abstract vertical profile and the irregular geometry of the mountains behind them.

Since the first caves began to be occupied, their domestic character hasn't changed. Today, around 3,000 people live in 1,500 caves. The caves, once a symbol of miserable living conditions, are today being converted into hotels, resorts, and restaurants. If their function is slowly changing, they still look the same, a testimony to the capacity of humans to artificialize nature (fig. 3.07).

A similar condition is found in Tunisia, where over time the Berbers of Matmata—a small village in the south—have been living underground to protect themselves from the hot climate. The village is organized around a cluster of underground dwellings, recognizable from afar by their sunken courtyards. Their history is not completely known. Some scholars date the origin of these houses to the Roman era, when two tribes were sent to colonize the Matmata region after one of the Punic wars.

Fig. 3.07. Guadix, Andalusia: striking contrast between the abstract verticality of the cave houses' chimneys and the dry surrounding landscape

Another theory relates to the Arab invasions. When Berbers felt more secure, they decided to move down from their homes in the mountains to this narrow area between Tunisia and Libya, where summer temperatures can reach 120°F. The decision to build underground was dictated by political, climatic, and soil conditions. Loess, a wind-deposited material composed of clay and gypsum, is a stable but pliable construction material.

In contrast to Guadix and Mediterranean settlements, the Matmata dwellings were not carved from the mountain but were literally dug into the ground around a sunken patio. Courtyards are normally semicircular, and their diameter can vary from 15 to 30 feet, with an average height of 32 feet. The rooms are about 15 feet wide, 25 to 30 feet long, and 9 feet high, their ceilings vaulted to bear the soil load. The number of the rooms for each house depended on the family size, but storage and granary rooms were always part of the house. In the middle of the courtyard, a cistern collected rainwater. These houses were revealed to the world only in 1976, when they were flooded by intense rains and the inhabitants were forced to seek help. A new village was built a few kilometers away from these historical settlements, but only a few families moved there. Today Matmata is a tourist

Fig. 3.08. Matmata, Tunisia: view from the sunken courtyard. *Courtesy of Tanya Dedyukhina*

destination, although since the 2011 Arab Spring, the number of visitors has diminished (fig. 3.08).

China also has a history of dwellings designed around a hole in the ground, especially in the Northeast in Shanxi, Shaanxi, Henan, Ningxia, and Gansu. Here it's estimated that thirty-five million people still live in cave houses called *yaodong*, which date to the Bronze Age.[2] The spatial logic of *yaodongs* mainly responds to bioclimatic conditions so that they remain cool in the hot summers and relatively warm in wintertime. Cave temperatures range between 50°F and 72°F and relative humidity is 30–75 percent. Belowground buildings are also protected from sand-blowing winds coming from Siberia and Mongolia.

The *yaodong* typically consists of underground rooms arranged around a rectangular, 22-foot-deep depression in the ground, with trees planted to provide shade. In some areas such as northern Shaanxi, every family has three to five caves; parents or grandparents live in the central main residence (fig. 3.09).

Fig. 3.09. Henan, China: a traditional *yaodong*. *Courtesy of Kevin Poh*

The most impressive collection of single *yaodong* units is in the city of Sanmenxia, in the country's central Henan Province, where more than 10,000 underground homes make up hundreds of microvillages. Seen from above, the precise holes in the ground create an abstract figure/ground pattern, similar to those Arab villages and North African urban structures whose porosity influenced many Western architects in the 1960s.[3] The bathroom, living room, and bedrooms look out on a courtyard roughly 27 feet deep. According to the *Daily Mail*, you can rent a three-bedroom house for $37 a month or purchase one for $56,000[4] (fig. 3.10).

The dwellings in all these regions share three characteristics. They have an informal and spontaneous character, the hot climate is a driving factor in their design, and they occur where soil conditions are favorable for digging. Many of the caves have plastered walls, and ceilings are vaulted or arched to reinforce the structure.

Fig. 3.10. Sanmenxia, Henan Province. Photo from *Architecture Without Architects: A Short Introduction to Non-Pedigreed Architecture,* by Bernard Rudofsky (New York: Museum of Modern Art, 1964).

ANCIENT RITES AND RITUALS

Underworld spaces have also served as places of resistance and often involve self-surveillance. Catacombs were clandestine structures built out of the rock and were used for protection from religious persecution. In Naples we find the Catacombs of San Gennaro; likely originally the tomb of a noble family, they became a shelter for the local Paleo-Christian community that fled Roman persecution. Their oldest catacomb dates to the third or fourth century, and their name comes from the city's patron, San Gennaro, who was arrested in the fourth century for professing Christianity and beheaded in 305 CE. In the fifth century his remains were transferred to the catacombs.

This structure—now open to the public—was developed on two levels plus an underground basilica, dedicated to St. Agrippinus, where an altar and a bishop's chair are preserved. Roughly 3,000 burials have been found, and their diversity allowed archeologists to reconstruct the social composition of the Neapolitan population. Whereas the simplest graves were just dug in the ground, the tombs of the wealthy classes—the *arcosolia*—were arched and decorated with frescoes or mosaics (fig. 03.11).

Fig. 3.11. Catacombs of San Gennaro, Naples: view of the hypogeous structure. *Courtesy of Dominik Matus*

The Underworld often celebrates death and ancient rituals and can even manifest the difficult relationship between religion and superstition, faith and reason. Such dichotomies are clearly expressed in another Neapolitan structure, the cemetery of Fontanelle. Located inside quarry caves from the Greek and Roman eras, Fontanelle cemetery is not only a cave, a moment of decompression in one of the densest areas of the city. It is also a space of devotion and pagan folklore. Originally imagined as an ossuary—a temporary burial place when church yards and crypts began to overflow—it held around 40,000 bodies, starting from the plague of 1656 and continuing until 1930. The burial ground quickly turned into something else—a bridge between life and death—as a cult of adopting skulls began to develop. Neapolitans were assigned to take care of specific remains in return for favors. In 1969, the Roman Catholic Church closed the cemetery to stop these activities (fig. 3.12).

In France, too, the need to bury the dead led to the construction of an extensive network of tombs: the Catacombs of Paris. Starting in the eighteenth century, when traditional cemeteries

Fig. 3.12. Cemetery of Fontanelle, Naples: faith and folklore. *Courtesy of Dominik Matus*

were overflowing and conditions became unhygenic, around six million Parisians' bones found a resting place in the underground. Some of the quarry tunnels that had populated Paris's underground since Roman times were converted into ossuaries that went on for 200 miles, 65 feet below the earth surface. Cemeteries began to be emptied in 1786, beginning with the largest one, Les Innocents. It took about ten years to move all the bones into the catacombs. From the French Revolution onward, the dead were buried directly in these ossuaries, and in stacking bones, a sort of romantic-grotesque atmosphere was created, in part by mining engineer Louis-Étienne Héricart de Thury, who oversaw some of the renovation work.

Finally, in 1860, the city put a stop to this practice. Over the years, the catacombs have been occupied, reused, and vandalized. During World War II, the Nazis built a bunker there, and in 2004 police discovered a movie theater in one of the caverns. Today only a small part of this complex is open to the public (fig. 3.13).

Outside Europe, an interesting exploration of the Underworld as a continuation of life after death comes from Chinese imperial

Fig. 3.13. Catacombs of Paris: underground and necrophilia. *Courtesy of Shadowgate*

tombs. In their long history, every dynasty built its own palaces and tombs. The Ming and Qing imperial tombs—from the fourteenth to the twentieth centuries—are located in settings carefully chosen according to the principles of geomancy or feng shui to ensure harmony between humans and their environment. They were typically designed as a sequence of buildings, monuments, and sculptures that support ceremonies and rituals. They commemorated the emperor's authority, political power, and actions, but also his immortality or presence in the afterlife.

The tomb of the first Ming emperor, the Xiaoling Tomb in Nanjing, dictated the basic principles for the design of subsequent imperial tumuli, or burial mounds, in Beijing and other regions. For example, Changling Tomb, built for the third emperor Zhu Di and his spouse Xu, is 31 miles from Beijing. Built in 1409, it is part of a 30-acre natural area. An arched gate marks the entrance to this complex, where three main buildings are aligned along a longitudinal axis. The destination is the City of Treasure, a 985-foot-diameter circular wall made of two components: Baoding—the mound above the burial chamber—and Xuangong,

the actual burial chamber. It's here, within the 23-foot-high city walls, that Emperor Zhu Di was buried (fig. 3.14).

Fig. 3.14. Changling Tomb, Beijing. *Photo: Alfons von Mumm*

In contrast to Changling, Dingling is famous for its underground palace, the only subterranean mausoleum among the Ming dynasty's thirteen imperial tombs. Built between 1584 and 1590, Dingling is the tomb of the thirteenth emperor, Zhu Yijun. In 1956 archeologists began trial excavations with the possibility of one day studying the largest Ming mausoleum, Changling. Excavations were completed in 1957, and when experts reached this underground tomb 88 feet below the ground, they found not only an incredible architectural space containing five vaulted halls, but also coffins, thrones, and a rich collection of precious objects: porcelain, textiles, and silk. In addition, all of the inner wooden chamber doors were still intact. In 1959, a museum was opened. After the Dingling's project, Chinese law prohibited further excavations on historical sites, and the plan to use Dingling as a prototype archeological site was abandoned (fig. 3.15).

Fig. 3.15. Dingling Tomb: view of the underground palace. *Courtesy of CE Photo, Uwe Aranas*

BACK TO THE EARTH

If today's transformative Underworld spaces are typically the realm of wealthy classes, in some parts of the world they are a repository of social marginalization and poverty. From Bogotá to New York and Nairobi, people have periodically colonized landfills, sewers, and underground passageways in the absence of any decent alternative.

In Bucharest, for example, more than 6,000 homeless people live in a system of tunnels that run beneath the Romanian capital. This network, created by the former president Nicolae Ceaușescu, was intended to centrally heat the city center. Bucharest's underground doesn't have any particular architectural interest, or a specific spatial design that makes living there attractive. It's just desperation and social disconnection that have produced its massive occupation in recent years. Steam pipes make the tunnels hot and humid, and they are populated by a suffering humanity. Most of the residents, raised in orphanages opened during the Communist era and recently dismantled, suffer from HIV, tuberculosis, hepatitis, and drug addiction. This segregated population's abuse of Aurolac, a silver paint inhaled through plastic bags, made the tunnels infamous. In 2015 police evicted some of the residents by sealing one of the entrances (fig. 3.16).

On the opposite end of the spectrum are Underworld domestic spaces that address environmental issues, climate change, and sustainability. Architects reinterpret archaic typologies to establish a dialogue with their context, optimize costs, save energy, and experiment with a more frugal way of living.

One example is Casa de Retiro Espiritual (House of Spiritual Retreat) in Seville, Spain, built in 1976–79 by Emilio Ambasz. It reinterprets traditional elements of Andalusian culture by using an eclectic language that blends topography, organic shapes, and orthogonal geometries, and it metaphorically reaches both the sky and the underground. Ambasz experimented with the tension between an iconic bifold wall that marks the house's presence in the landscape, and a sunken space—a nod to the Andalusian patio, an expression of the Arab culture that dominated Andalusia for centuries. The house is designed as a spatial procession starting with the bifold wall, which recalls the *atalayas*, observation towers built on the Iberian Peninsula to warn against enemy invasions. A balcony pays homage to the Arabic architectural tradition and to

Fig. 3.16. Biancoshock: Borderlife, Milan, 2016. Installation inspired by Bucharest underground. *Courtesy of Biancoshock*

the *mashrabiya*, wooden screens that protect women from indiscreet eyes. The *mashrabiya* becomes a panoramic terrace, the last stop in the process of ascension.

The patio contrasts with the vertical white walls and acts as a filter between the exterior and the cave house, made of concrete and bricks. Every room opens to the patio to take advantage of sunlight. The roof also takes cues from vernacular buildings; it is insulated with earth and grass to keep the interiors cool in the summertime. By rethinking tradition, the house addresses both local conditions and global concerns, offering a sustainable model of living that is based on a careful dialogue with its context.

Spanish architect Fernando Higueras also pushed the boundaries of architecture with his provocative Rascainfiernos, or Hellscraper, a subterranean house he designed for himself in Madrid. Disillusioned with modernist architecture, Higueras had always looked to the vernacular to find inspiration, and here he played with the romantic idea of an innovative cave providing comfort and refuge.

The starting point was a two-story detached house he bought in 1972 just before his divorce. Higueras designed an inverted skyscraper in the garden so he could essentially keep living with his wife and five sons. Light was the main element driving the design. Four 6.5-foot-square skylights illuminate a dramatic void nearly 23 feet belowground. Built on two levels, the first, 870-square-foot underground level contains the bedroom and living room. The second, 645-square-foot underground level houses bathrooms and a studio. By applying the lesson of informal vernacular architecture, Higueras was able to maintain an average indoor temperature between 61°F and 79°F, which made mechanical heating and cooling almost unnecessary. The construction methods were also somewhat primitive. A 30-by-30-foot hole in the ground was dug with a pick and shovel, since there was no room for machines. Since 2008, when the architect died, the cave has been occupied by the Fernando Higueras Foundation (fig. 3.17).

In 2009, in the Graubünden Canton, Switzerland, Christian Müller and Bjarne Mastenbroek from the Dutch firm SeARCH experimented with traditional Alpine architecture in Villa Vals, a house that disappears into the landscape. An old stone and wooden barn was preserved and used as the entrance to the house, and a 72-foot-long tunnel connected the barn to a house that was excavated into the mountain. A semicircular inclined patio hints at the house inside the hill and forms a facade clad in a traditional material—Valser quartzite recovered from the site. Irregular openings

Fig. 3.17. Rascainfiernos, Madrid: an artificial cave. *Courtesy of Fundación Fernando Higueras*

allow light to penetrate the interior. On the first floor are the living room, kitchen, and a double-height library, while the second floor contains bedrooms. The house's interior massing reveals the complexity of the space. Every room is on a different level: the bedrooms, rather than being enclosed and connected by a corridor, work as open platforms that permit multiple uses and offer different views of the Alps. In its collage of spaces and playful interactions between old and new, nature and architecture, and Cartesian and organic geometries, Villa Vals questions the conventional Alpine architecture of pitched roofs and monolithic structures, and also the cold, abstract precision of modernist Swiss architecture (fig. 3.18).

Exploring the domestic possibilities of the Underworld can lead to materials that trigger emotional and psychological responses: not only light, but color, sound, and water. Starting in the second half of the twentieth century, phenomenology has become a central aspect of architecture. With this lens, we can look into a secret and mysterious space: Casa Gilardi, a house designed by the Mexican architect Luis Barragán in 1976.

Situated in the Federal District of Mexico, this house was Barragán's last project, a synthesis of his spatial ideas. Casa Gilardi is a combination of two abstract volumes organized around an existing jacaranda tree that the architect transformed into a centripetal force in his composition. From the street, the building's pink facade hints at the house's colorful interior planes. The main house contains a kitchen and bathroom downstairs, a living room and study on the middle level, and two bedrooms on the upper floor. The second volume is a metaphysical swimming pool, which

Fig. 3.18. Villa Vals, Switzerland: view of the entire housing complex. *Courtesy of Kecko*

his clients envisioned as a space for entertaining. It's connected to the main house with a yellow corridor. Perforated on one side by ribbonlike openings, the corridor acts as a threshold between private and public life, and between routine and pleasure.

The swimming pool is an atemporal space containing very few elements. The colors used here are a direct reference to the painter Chucho Reyes Ferreira, who's been called the Mexican Marc Chagall, yet indirect light from the roof system of skylights constantly changes the perceptions of color and space. A column sunk into the pool is not load bearing but simply there to attract light and change the physical proportions of the space. In contrast to the solid brick exterior walls, the interior is a hidden refuge from everyday life. This approach, which recalls the European avant-garde movements of the twentieth century—suprematism and neo-plasticism—and the Mexican painting tradition—Diego Rivera and Frida Kahlo, above all—combines abstraction and sensualism in a unique way that inspired contemporary artists such as James Turrell, who spent a month in the house studying Barragán's work[5] (fig. 3.19).

Fig. 3.19. Casa Gilardi, Mexico City: colors, light, and water

Fig. 3.20. La Fábrica: view from the cathedral. *Courtesy of Forgemind ArchiMedia*

When personal and collective memories merge, a home environment can combine different, even contradictory, cues. In that sense the Underworld can be manifest not just as a physical condition but as a creative tension. An example is La Fábrica (the Factory), where the Catalan architect Ricardo Bofill repurposed an abandoned cement factory composed of silos, 2.5 miles of subterranean tunnels, and machine rooms.

Originally built in phases, the factory was a collection of additions with no unifying logic. The architect took advantage of this condition by inserting a new program completely disconnected from the building's brutalist volumes. Starting in 1973, Bofill transformed the entire factory into his atelier and private residence. Eight of the thirty silos were preserved, and by tearing

down the remaining silos, Bofill reduced the factory to a more domestic scale that is nevertheless severe and austere. The preserved silos were converted into a library, laboratory, archives, offices, media rooms, and a so-called Cathedral for hosting cultural events.

A concrete volume was transformed into the main living room that combines, in Bofill's words, "the domestic, monumental, brutalist, and conceptual."[6]. The lower floors house a kitchen and private living area. Over the years, nature has been allowed to take over, with eucalyptus, cypress, and other lush plants spilling from its roofs and partially hiding the concrete forms. Today La Fábrica remains unfinished, the object of constant transformation over a period of forty years (fig. 3.20).

FOUR

EMERGING FROM DARKNESS

In the final canto of Inferno, after a twenty-four-hour journey through Hell, Dante and the Roman poet Virgil leave this dark subterranean universe and climb toward the earth's surface. In emerging at the antipodes, the other side of the world, Dante concludes the first part of his Divine Comedy:

"E quindi uscimmo a riveder le stelle" (From there we came out to see once more the stars).[1]

Stars, the bridge between hell and purgatory, indicate a new direction: a push toward knowledge and wisdom. As seen in the previous chapters, to deeply understand the functioning of our cities and homes, a purely two-dimensional approach seems superficial. Only a three-dimensional section can reveal the hidden layers and, consequently, the relationship between aboveground and belowground domains. While in the past the physical separation between these two realms was evident—and their complementary aspects imagined but never explicitly explored—today we can look at our cities as continuous vertical entities that metaphorically reach from the sky to the center of the earth.

In contrast with the incessant edification of new buildings that still characterize not only the Western world but especially emerging countries, the Underworld can be reused and adapted to new purposes. Some of its spaces—traditionally confined to a secret dimension—have finally emerged from darkness and have officially been recognized as functional parts of city life.

Reusing, recycling, and transforming become design acts. To give the Underworld a new life, to open it up to the community, means to activate a process of unveiling.

Culture can be a reason for bringing the Underworld to light. Zeitz MOCAA—Museum of Contemporary African Art—is an adaptive reuse of the Grain Silo Complex, once the tallest building in Cape Town, South Africa, which includes a grading tower and forty-two silos. The new program consists of 65,000 square feet containing eighty galleries in a five-story space. A bookshop, restaurant, and reading rooms were also inserted. Thomas Heatherwick Studio preserved the entire complex but carved out the silos with a curvilinear plane to create an atrium and expose the interior for public use. Each silo was reinforced on the inside with a 9-inch-thick, poured-in-place concrete sleeve. Traces of this excavation process are visible: the edges of the cut tubes are polished to contrast with the old concrete's irregular surface.

Fig. 4.01. Zeitz MOCAA, Cape Town: sectioned tubes become a full-height atrium. *Photo: Iwan Baan*

The atrium's void serves a space of decompression for the new program, since it creates a gap between two dense areas of the building: the grading tower and the five floors of permanent and temporary exhibitions.

The silos, lit from above both naturally and artificially, act as a landmark—a postindustrial lighthouse for the surrounding harbor. Except for the atrium, the existing complex maintains its original section, based on the repetition of identical floors (fig. 4.01). A dichotomy is therefore evident: inside, the atrium introduces a new architectural language and a moment of discontinuity in the overall experience of the space; outside, the grading tower's severe image is a reminder of its original function as a place of production and labor. In the cityscape, one can still read traces of its past.

A similar project is the Palais de Tokyo in Paris, a modern art center that opened in 1937 and was abandoned after the completion of the Pompidou Centre in the 1970s. In the renovation, French architects Lacaton & Vassal applied a clear intervention strategy. Rather than adding new volumes or otherwise altering the original building, they worked by subtraction, gradually liberating it from the superfluous decorative layers that had been added over time. But they preserved and highlighted the original patinaed surfaces, essentially treating time as a material.

Rather than following a prescribed circulation route, visitors are free to explore the whole building as they wish, from the cave-like basement to the upper-level exhibit spaces. Palais de Tokyo is a supporting backdrop that only suggests ways to engage with the artworks. Subtle cues such as ramps, slope variations, doors, and staircases act as thresholds or boundaries. By recycling and modifying forms and reinterpreting existing messages, architecture can establish a dialogue with other disciplines and promote user participation (fig. 4.02).

In Shenzhen, China, O-Office and Marc Maurer Architects imbued an abandoned structure with the dynamics, density, and patterns of the urban environment. In transforming it into exhibition and event spaces, the designers focused their attention on two steel silos 18 feet in diameter, four concrete silos 50 feet in diameter, and a vertical transportation tower—just a fragment of the 10-acre factory complex. These components form a 250-foot-long building made out of transparent and lightweight elements such as bridges, ramps, vertical connectors, and horizontal platforms. The result is a journey through hidden spaces that takes visitors deep inside the silos. The raw interior materials—including pipes, tubes, and equipment—are left exposed, and the insertion of glass and white uniform surfaces contrasts with the silos' brutalist language. Strategic openings in the floor open sight lines and break down the rigidity of the industrial floor plans. This project explores two main ideas: one is the continuity of the building's interior circulation with the surrounding urban environment. The other one is a process of gradual revealing formerly inaccessible spaces and transforming them for collective use. Even industrial silos can become active participants in urban life rather than simply remnants of a recent past (fig. 4.03).

Fig. 4.02. Palais de Tokyo, Paris. *Courtesy of Jean-Daniel Pauget*

Fig. 4.03. Shenzhen silo conversion: view from the circular stairs. *Courtesy of Maurer United Architects*

MEMORY AND SYMBOLISM

Memory plays a central role in exposing the Underworld to urban life. In the Netherlands, the clapboard house of SS commander Albert Konrad Gemmeker is the only building left of the Nazi transit camp at Westerbork—a detention center opened in 1939 to temporarily hold Romani and Dutch Jews. Every Tuesday, trains transported them to exterminations camps in Poland, Czech Republic, and Germany. It's estimated that around 10,000 people passed through this complex.

The Commander House was declared a national monument in 1994, and in 2015, Oving Architekten was commissioned to formalize the memorial. The firm froze the building in time, isolating it in a protective glass skin, and visitors enter through a new opaque volume at the back of the house. This narrow, L-shaped corridor contains a pantry, storage, and bathrooms. Visitors access the Commander House through this compressed space, and the void between the house and its glass envelope can accommodate up to one hundred people during exhibitions and conferences. In establishing the importance of architecture as historical testimony, Oving Architekten elevated a decayed wooden house to the status of a monument open to collective remembrance (fig. 4.04).

Another horrific Underworld narrative was brought into the light at Quai de la Fosse, a 2012 memorial to the abolition of slavery in Nantes, France, designed by artist Krzysztof Wodiczko and architect Julian Bonder. In the eighteenth century, Nantes was France's most active slave port. More than 40 percent of the entire French slave trade was carried out in the city, and roughly 500,000 African slaves were hauled through the seaport on their way to America. Only in the 1990s did the city begin to confront its shameful past. In 1998, the 150th anniversary of the abolition of slavery, the city council decided to build a commemorative site on the riverbank. Quai de la Fosse consists of two levels: a street-level walk along the riverbank that connects to the History Museum and the different port sites, and a lower level symbolic of the ocean and stories of sorrow and desperation. There, a dimly lit corridor reminds us of the conditions in which slaves crossed the seas, trapped and compressed in the decks of the ships. The corridor—part of the Loire embankment in the nineteenth and twentieth centuries—was transformed as a wood gallery in which 1,710 opaque glass panels tell the slave trade story in fifty languages. By commemorating a

Fig. 4.04. Westerbork transit camp, Netherlands: exterior view of the Commander House. *Courtesy of OVING Architekten; photo: Susan Schuls*

dark period of slavery and colonialism, the memorial reclaims the banks of the Loire as a political act (fig. 4.05).

Sometimes the design program requires architects to reinterpret traditional building typologies or invent new ones. That was the case at the Netherlands Institute for Sound and Vision in Hilversum, designed by the Dutch office Neutelings Riedijk in 2006. Commissioned to design a vast national radio-and-television archives, the architects conceived the whole building as a modern-day necropolis—a subterranean world populated by people and information, where irony, metaphor, and spatial inversion were the guiding themes.

The structure houses audio and video archives, offices, labs and workshop areas, and museum spaces. These four main areas

Memory

Fig. 4.05. Quai de la Fosse, memorial to the abolition of slavery, Nantes, France: the subterranean passageway. *Courtesy of Groume*

Fig. 4.06. Netherlands Institute for Sounds and Vision, Hilversum: the atrium separates public functions from the underground necropolis. *Courtesy of Husky*

are grouped around a central void like a floating inverted ziggurat. The void is a public atrium, a transition between the aboveground program and the Underworld. The archives, on five underground levels, work as *memento mori*—an archeological stratum of memories and stories.[2] Aboveground exhibition and museum areas represent life—a place for events and social interaction.

The institute symbolizes the duality of life and death, matter and information, interior and exterior, past and present. The transparent facades, designed by Jaap Drupsteen, depict historical stills of Dutch television. The facades suggest the formal unity of the interior and, at the same time, evoke the immaterial character of data. The overall result is an ephemeral mosaic portraying the Dutch collective memory (fig. 4.06).

BUILDING CONNECTIONS

In the preservation-transformation of Castelgrande in Bellinzona, Switzerland (1981–2000), architect Aurelio Galfetti combined architecture, city, and landscape as a category of the Underworld. Asked to redevelop the historic fortress, the Swiss architect rejected the idea of the castle as an isolated object and instead connected it to the surrounding elements: a park, a lake, and the city. In integrating these fragments, Galfetti made Castelgrande the climax of a public promenade.[3]

The fortress, built on an jagged granite ridge, was used from the Neolithic era to the nineteenth century. During that time it served different functions—as a refuge from the Ticino River flooding, a castle, and a prison—but for most of its history it had been disconnected from the community. By digging vertical connections into the granite, Galfetti established a direct link between the lower parking area in the city and the castle's peak.

A sense of discovery leads visitors through the fortress's mysterious spaces. A long, dark tunnel ends at a concrete circular space fitted with lifts and staircases. After ascending 130 feet inside the rock, visitors reach the light at the top of the fortress. A ramp takes them to Castelgrande's original courtyard, now a terrace with panoramic views. A restaurant, conference halls, and exhibition areas were also added. Through the design of invisible elements, Galfetti reframed the fortress in relation to the surroundings and emphasized the spatial and natural qualities of the historic structure (fig. 04.07).

The Maritime Museum of Denmark, completed by BIG in 2013, illustrates something similar. This underground structure is strategically located between two major buildings: the Kronborg Castle—a UNESCO World Heritage site known from Shakespeare's *Hamlet*—and the Culture Yard, a new center in Helsingør, 30 miles from Copenhagen. In acting as a barycentric node between these two buildings, the Maritime Museum serves as public space that supports Kulturhavn Kronborg's initiatives to bring cultural attractions to Helsingør's harbor.

The starting point of the project was a sixty-year-old dry dock with 5-foot-thick walls and an 8-foot-thick floor. The dock was turned into an outdoor courtyard around which

Fig. 4.07. Castelgrande, Bellinzona: a tunnel excavated in the granite rock connects the city with the fortress. *Courtesy of Antonella Profeta*

Fig. 4.08. Maritime Museum of Denmark, Helsingør: the dock as scar of the past. *Courtesy of News Øresund*

the museum's main attractions revolve. Galleries lie 23 feet below the ground, accessed over a series of transversal bridges. These bridges have specific functions: one accommodates the flow of visitors in the museum; the other serves as an auditorium and connects the Maritime Museum with the castle.

The steel bridges were produced on a Chinese wharf and transported to Denmark on the biggest ship that had ever docked in Helsingør. It is ironic that even after the site stopped functioning as a dock, it contains latent traces of its maritime past (fig. 4.08).

Sometimes the Underground offers a chance to insert a new architectural vocabulary into a historic center while avoiding complicated juxtapositions or too-obvious associations with its surroundings. When CLEAA Studio (Claudio Lucchin & Architetti Associati) expanded the Hannah Arendt School of Social Profession, in the historic Capuchin Convent in Bolzano, Italy, they addressed this issue, as well as how technology could improve the building's performance in terms of comfort, functionality, and resource efficiency. CLEAA went 55 feet underground to create four levels composed of nine classrooms, six workshops, utility rooms, a winter garden, and small study niches.

At 21,500 square feet, the layout revolves around a subterranean atrium that captures daylight, acts as a main gathering space, piques the curiosity of bystanders above, and reveals the building's interior logic. Geometrically integrated into the existing

school complex, the atrium ceiling is the only visible element of the new building. An underground corridor on the first level connects the old school with the reinforced-concrete addition. Its walls are irregular, deformed, and covered with a plaster spray layer that keeps out radon gas. Although all the spaces are below city level, its materials are diaphanous, with glass interior walls that contrast with the cave-like atmosphere.

Technology plays a central role in the building's environmental performance. The Hannah Arendt School is equipped with a mechanical ventilation system that circulates air through ceiling diffusers and grills. Artificial lighting is controlled by neon sensors, whose temperature and color reacts to the time of the day and outside weather conditions. By playing up the dichotomy between old visible volumes and new hidden structures, CLEAA achieved a delicate balance—and without leaving an egotistical trace of their presence (fig. 4.09).

Fig. 4.09. Hannah Arendt School, Bolzano: view of the addition. *Courtesy of CLEAA (Claudio Lucchin & Architetti Associati); photo: Giacomo Flaim*

PUSHING BOUNDARIES: REUSE AND IRONY

War, with its atrocities and endless wake of sorrow, inspired the design of the underground nightclub B018 in Beirut. In it, Lebanese architect Bernard Khoury explored the thin line between life and death and the relationship between tragedy and irony.

In 1998, B018 was moved from a different part of the city to Karantina, adjacent to the Beirut port. Karantina was famous for its turbulent history, having been a refugee camp for Palestinians and Kurds, and also because in 1976 during the civil war, about 1,500 people were massacred there. After that, the area was fenced off and the camps demolished.

Khoury's strategy was to address head-on the harsh realities of war. The nightclub is a hypogeous structure similar to a communal grave. Its roof, the only visible facade, is composed of a moving steel structure with Plexiglas mirrors that can be lifted hydraulically to reveal the dance floor below, transforming it into an outdoor discotheque. The roof is inscribed into a circular concrete ring with parking spaces arranged around it. People, cars, and the retractable metal structure—nothing is static or fixed. The result is an endless motion, a counterpart to the building's presence. In the background is Beirut's dense skyline. When the roof is closed, the concrete disk recalls a

Fig. 4.10. B018, Beirut: the underground structure inscribed in a helicopter pad. *Courtesy of DW5 BERNARD KHOURY*

helicopter pad. A staircase leads to the main space, where backless sofas resemble scattered coffins and double as dance platforms.

By inserting an entertainment program into such a traumatized site, Khoury made irony a driving agent: rather than a rhetorical reminiscence, B018 is playful and antimonumental, a celebration of Lebanese nightlife and club culture. It's an attempt to look at Lebanon's recent history through the disenchanted symbols traditionally associated with war—the bunker, the helicopter, the grave. Although it was initially slated to be a temporary structure, B018 soon became the emblem of Beirut's postwar rebirth, and twenty years later the nightclub is still there (fig. 4.10).

As technology evolves, increasing numbers of caves are being converted into comfortable public places that nurture social interaction and communication. In 2011 Studio Stratum designed the first underground post office building in the world. The Postojna cave in Slovenia has been used by humans since the seventeenth century and is now a famous concert hall.

Imagined as a sinuous glass pavilion with open-plan exhibit and retail areas, the serpentine structure adapts to the cave's irregular contours, and its transparent facade has four entrances. By contrast, the service areas and sanitary facilities are hidden, introverted, and opaque. The building incorporates innovative heating and ventilation systems and an underground biological treatment plant. Construction materials were transported to the site on a small train and assembled by hand, and the same railway connects it to the city.

By juxtaposing the primordial character of the Postojna cave with the ephemeral glass pavilion, Studio Stratum used the Underworld as a laboratory for testing construction methods and technical innovations (fig. 4.11).

SACRED SPACES

In the process of emerging from a hidden past, the Underworld is often associated with transforming religious structures into secular spaces. This conversion implies a double shift: functional and conceptual. In some of the projects shown here, the building preserves its aura or immaterial uniqueness while opening its doors to a new relationship with the outside world.

In Maastricht, Netherlands, the bookseller chain Selexyz asked the firm Merkx + Girod Architects to design a new store in the thirteenth-century Dominican church, a Gothic structure built in 1294 by the Order of Predicators. The church had been subject to many changes during its troubled history: closed and confiscated by Napoleon Bonaparte in 1794, it was used as a warehouse, an archive, and even a bicycle shed. Working within its 8,000 square feet, in 2007 Merkx + Girod Architects designed 13,000 square feet of retail space. Rather than adding new floors, which would have radically altered the church's appearance and spatial continuity, the architects designed a three-story blackened-steel book stack that holds roughly 45,000 volumes. The stack incorporates an elevator and stairs, and, once on top, visitors can get a closer look at the restored frescoes on the vault.

The bookshelves' vertical and horizontal circulation establishes a visual and physical contact with the old structure—in fact, some of the existing columns in the longitudinal nave have been incorporated into the design. And by shifting the bookshelf toward the lateral nave, the Gothic space was preserved and honored. The firm also designed niches for an information desk, cash registers, magazine stands, and a café (fig. 4.12).

Whereas the Dominican church was repurposed primarily by adding a single macro piece of furniture, a project in Santpedor, Spain, brought the Underworld to light with a surgical graft. Asked to transform an eighteenth-century church into a cultural center in 2011, architect David Closes was tasked with adapting a remnant ruin at the Sant Francesc Convent, built by Franciscan priests between 1721 and 1729. In 2000 the convent was demolished, and what remained of the church was saved and restored.

In adapting it as an auditorium, multipurpose space, and archive, the architect had one main goal: to preserve the main nave's character by highlighting its features with natural light. Closes achieved this with several skylights placed strategically in the apse, in the nave with views of the belfry, in the open main chapel, and at the entrance wall. The nave was preserved

Fig. 4.11. Underground post office, Postojna cave, Slovenia. *Courtesy of Studio Stratum; photo: Miran Kambič*

Fig. 4.12. Selexyz Dominicanen Bookstore, Maastricht: at the top of the bookshelf. *Courtesy of Bert Kaufmann*

Fig. 4.13. Convent de Sant Francesc, Spain: view of the vertical connections. *Courtesy of David Closes; photo: Jordi Surroca*

in its original condition, and the new program, which included toilets and equipment rooms, was moved outside as a semidetached, abstract volume that seems to float on the side of the church. Interior and exterior stairs link old and new volumes and connect the church with the upper floor of the side chapels, which were originally accessible only from the convent. The new entrance reads as an irregular glazed volume, a parasite hanging on the church's main facade and acting as a visual magnet (fig. 4.13).

A reverse process is on display at the Abbey of Our Lady of Nový Dvůr, designed by John Pawson in Bohemia, Czech Republic,

Fig. 4.14. Abbey of Our Lady of Nový Dvůr, Czech Republic. Courtesy of Abbey of Our Lady of Nový Dvůr

between 1999 and 2004, where conventional buildings were converted into a religious structure isolated from the outside world—an oasis of worship and labor. Pawson was given the commission by a monastery of Trappist monks—a branch of Cistercians that originated in France in the seventeenth century and spread throughout the world. They are normally cloistered, opening their monastery to outsiders only on the day of its consecration.[4]

Pawson's design assembled the various fragments—a ruined manor house, agricultural structures, farmland, a cemetery, and a forest—into a unified complex whose organization is dictated by ancient rituals: the monks' daily sequence of church services, private prayer, and reading. In addition to preserving these components, new volumes were added, such as a church, workshop spaces, and other facilities. In addressing the delicate threshold between spiritual and secular life, Pawson envisioned this project as a secret and inaccessible microcity that runs parallel to the world outside yet is completely isolated. From the cloister of the monastery, monks can see the cemetery, the final step of their journey in the pursuit of heaven (fig. 4.14).

FIVE

ON NATURE AND ARTIFICE

Fig. 5.01. Johann Bernhard Fischer von Erlach's imaginary view of Mount Athos, from *Entwurff einer historischen Architectur*, 1725.

In 1725, Johann Bernhard Fischer von Erlach depicted a series of mythological landscapes in *Entwurff einer historischen Architectur*[1] ("Project for a history of architecture"). In these engravings, nature is artificially reinvented: gardens, hills, and caves take on the look of petrified architecture. As such, they become objects of historical study in the same way as buildings, monuments, and sculpture. In the architect's vision, the dichotomy between nature and artifice evaporates (fig. 5.01). The engraving suggests that the Underworld, with its secret and hidden spaces, is both a natural and cultural condition—the result of an intricate dialogue among culture, topography, and geology. Indeed, in the last twenty years a growing awareness of ecology and the potential of digital technologies has led to new possibilities. In the following projects, whether historical or modern, nature has been absorbed to varying degrees into an architectural framework. Many reject the traditional dichotomy between architecture and nature,[2] interior and exterior, public and private, sacred and secular.

CARVING, DIGGING, MODELING

One of the most impressive examples of the ambiguity between architecture and nature is in China's Henan Province, where the erosive action of rivers and winds created a unique environment—the Longmen Grottoes. The Yi River shapes a valley whose riverbanks have been used over the centuries to build caves and niches; the earliest were carved out in the fifth and sixth centuries. While the eastern bank was used mainly for dwellings, on the western bank more than 2,000 caves were excavated and 110,000-some Buddhist statues and 2,800 inscriptions were found. These limestone cliffs have yielded an extraordinary showcase of Chinese art from the Northern Wei and Tang dynasties (316–907 CE), and historians have been able to reconstruct their stylistic evolution since the fifth century.

The Longmen Grottoes have been looted over the years, especially during the Sino-Japanese War, and several statues are now in Japanese museums. However, since 1951, the artwork on site has been systematically surveyed. A weather station was also opened to monitor environmental conditions and plan preservation work. Today, pedestrian paths have made the entire site accessible, and in 2000, Longmen Grottoes became a UNESCO World Heritage site (fig. 5.02).

In Ethiopia, traditional-looking religious buildings were remarkably carved out of bedrock and shaped with tools like pieces

Fig. 5.02. Longmen Grottoes, China: view from the eastern bank of the Yi River. *Courtesy of Ryan McFarland*

of sculpture. An exceptional example is Lalibela, located in the Amhara region, 400 miles from Addis Ababa at an elevation of 8,200 feet. Lalibela was founded in the twelfth century as a New Jerusalem—an answer to the Muslim conquest of the sacred city in 1187. Eleven monolithic churches were erected using massive blocks hewn from the surrounding volcanic tuff rocks. These blocks were then refined to shape architectural elements such as portals, openings, and columns. The churches are grouped in two clusters: a northern group consisting of five churches and an eastern group with another five. The eleventh church, Bet Giyorgis, stands alone.

Trenches and ceremonial passages connect the eleven churches with an invisible system of caves and catacombs. Coptic Christians have made pilgrimages here since the twelfth century, and the churches are still used daily. Every morning a service is held in each building, and every year 80,000 to 100,000 visitors arrive. A unique aspect of these structures is that they were built from the top down. Their sunken condition partially reveals the history and construction methods of each church; rather than serving as visible landmarks, these sunken structures are scars, traces of a spiritual community that projects its identity down in the underground. In that way the Lalibela churches act as a gate between life—the earth's surface—and death, the catacombs (fig. 5.03).

In Coober Pedy, Australia, a similar kind of space was dug 10 to 55 feet belowground. This small city between Alice Springs and Adelaide was founded in 1915, when opal was discovered and the first mines were opened. In a few years this desert landscape became the largest opal-mining region in the world. At the end of the 1990s, there were more than 250,000 mine entrances. In 1993 local miners built the Serbian Orthodox Church, carving it out of the sandstone. Because of the heat, it is entirely subterranean, including a community hall, religious school, and parish house. Coober Pedy has became a popular tourist destination, and recently underground motels were added (fig. 5.04).

The quest for isolation, silence, and solitude has motivated the subterranean construction of monasteries and religious complexes. In Amorgos, the easternmost of the Cycladic Islands, is the Monastery of Hozoviotissa, nestled in a rock cliff 980 feet above the Aegean Sea. From a distance it looks like a white abstract wall with small perforations. It was built in the eleventh century to house an icon of the Virgin Mary that had miraculously arrived from Palestine under mysterious circumstances. A long, steep series of stairs lead to the monastery, which is roughly 130 feet

Fig. 5.03. Bet Giyorgis church, Lalibela, Ethiopia. *Courtesy of Armin Hamm*

long and only 16 feet wide. Eight floors connected by narrow passages accommodate a church, cells, dining room, storage rooms, and ovens (fig. 5.06).

These vernacular expressions of collective architecture are examples of what Bernard Rudofsky called architecture without architects,[3] blending nature and architecture according to formal solutions that today can appear extreme. An example of an entirely different approach is Finland's Temppeliaukio Church, a Lutheran temple in Helsinki. The result of a competition in 1961, the church was built by Timo and Tuomo Suomalainen inside a massive block of granite in the middle of a dense residential area. If the rock-hewn churches in Ethiopia were built top down, Temppeliaukio is built inside out, excavated into the rock. Visitors are directed into the church on a smooth and continuous pathway. Inside is a grand oval dome made out of copper plates and attached to the rock's irregular surfaces with 180 glass panels that allow natural light to penetrate the sanctuary.

Fig. 5.04. Coober Pedy church, Australia: interior view

From outside, the dome seems to float, and the glass reduces its impact on the surroundings. Concrete beams support the 8-foot-diameter dome. The rock walls vary in height from 16 to 30 feet. The pulpit is made out of concrete, and the altar, placed on an ice-age crevice in the rock, is sawn granite. Water, which normally infiltrated the cracks, is channeled into ducts. Protected from prying eyes, completely absorbed in the city's mineral landscape, the church's acoustics make it a fantastic concert venue. Through sound, nature, and light, humans can establish a direct connection with God (fig. 5.05).

Fig. 5.05. Temppeliaukio Church, Helsinki: a cave topped by a copper dome. *Courtesy of Dennis Jarvis*

IMITATION AND CAMOUFLAGE

In some cases, the Underworld represents a moment of transition between tradition and innovation, vernacular expression and formal complexity. In Lanzarote, Canary Islands, the desire to fuse nature and culture is accompanied by a statement against the status quo. Starting in the late 1960s, the artist César Manrique embarked on a series of provocative alternatives to the cheaply

Fig. 5.06. Monastery of Hozoviotissa, Amorgos: a long, white wall. *Courtesy of Giorgio Martino*

built structures that littered Lanzarote and the Canary Islands to accommodate an influx of tourists.

In 1974, for example, Manrique's design collaboration with Eduardo Cáceres and Jesús Soto produced El Mirador, a panoramic café-bar overlooking the eight Canary Islands and the famous El Río, a strait separating Lanzarote and the small island of La Graciosa. Perched on top of a 1,300-foot cliff, the bar is invisible from the exterior and is part of an existing nineteenth-century military structure.

Manrique's intervention addresses the site's volcanic character and violent beauty while expressing the human desire to turn even the most impervious environment into inhabitable space. It was imagined as a primitive cave separated from the elements by a thin glass layer. Visitors approach El Mirador along a panoramic route, immersed in a lunar landscape of cavities, depressions, and craters. The main entrance is a narrow tunnel excavated into the rock that dramatically opens up in the café.

El Mirador is just a fragment dug and filled between sedimentary layers. Its doesn't try to compete with the spectacular setting, but simply to find a balance between nature and architecture (fig. 5.07).

A similar strategy can be seen in the Netherlands at Moses Bridge, an invisible passageway designed in 2011 by RO&AD Architecten. Moses Bridge is part of the West Brabant Water Line, which dates from the seventeenth century and almost disappeared. The bridge connects a hike-and-bike trail to Fort de Roovere across a shallow moat. By playfully appropriating the fairy imagery of castles, moats, and drawbridges, a slash of infrastructure became a submerged bridge surrounded by water and invisible from afar.

Because the existing moat was too shallow for boats, the designers conceived this "bridge" as a trench that disappears in the landscape without revealing its structure. From the distance, one can perceive only a scar in the walls of the moat and a thin presence on the water surface. To reach the fortress therefore implies walking below water level without getting wet. Moses Bridge is made of accoya wood, which has undergone an acetylation process that gives it a fifty-year lifespan aboveground and twenty-five years underwater. If invisible bridges historically helped enemies access and conquer the castle, today the Moses Bridge helps visitors enjoy one of the fortresses of the West Brabant Water Line (fig. 5.09).

In Italy, on the famous hills of Chianti, Tuscany, the Underworld was used to spectacular effect in the celebration of wine culture. At the famous Antinori Winery, which opened its doors in 2012,

Fig. 5.07. Mirador del Río, Lanzarote, Spain: view from the café. *Courtesy of Christian Freiherr von der Ropp*

Fig. 5.08. Antinori Winery, Tuscany: the terra-cotta vaults. *Courtesy of Massimo Castiello*

a 540,000-square-foot building is entirely buried in a hillside, a symbol of its deep-rooted ties to the land. Viewed from the road, it reveals its presence only by a slash of glazed facade on the brow of the hill, its curving and deeply cantilevered roof covered with grapevines. Inside, two horizontal cuts in the roof let in light and frame a view of the landscape. Two levels contain offices, a museum, a shop, and the glass-enclosed tasting rooms, which jut theatrically over the wine cellars. These vaulted terra-cotta caves are the most secret and controlled part of the building, where wine matures in barrels under ideal temperature conditions. The overall image is monumental, archaic, primitive, and metaphysical at the same time.

Grapes and visitors follow an opposite path inside and around the winery. Visitors ascend from the underground parking area on a sculptural corkscrew staircase. By contrast, the grapes descend from the point of arrival into the fermentation and bottling areas and then down to the caves. About 35 acres were excavated, a reminder that any landscape intervention, even the most respectful one, is a radical act of alteration (fig. 5.08).

The Solimene Factory, built in 1951 by the Italian architect Paolo Soleri, is an outstanding example of creating an interior landscape through metaphor. Owned by the family Solimene, famous for its tradition of ceramic craftsmanship, it sits in the small town of Vietri del Mare, on the Amalfi coast. The design was influenced by Soleri's education at Frank Lloyd Wright's Taliesin, which he attended in the late 1940s, and by the Italian baroque legacies of Francesco Borromini and Guarino Guarini.

The factory was built with local materials—terra-cotta tiles, irregular mosaic glass, and ceramics. While the facade is a playful collage of the circular bases of terra-cotta vases lacquered in different colors and embedded in the concrete cladding, the interior is completely excavated from the mountain. Five levels radiate from a central atrium, lit from above, and house not only the factory but also a showroom and residential units. A helicoidal ramp connects the different stages of ceramics production, similar to Wright's Guggenheim Museum in New York. This process moves vertically from the modeling of clay in the lathe to the decoration and subsequent firing. The ramp allows the pieces to be easily transported along the different levels.

In section, another singular aspect grabs attention: the pillars that support the ceiling form a sort of treelike structure, mimicking an artificial forest. This dendriform reference is just one of the several aspects of the project: the Solimene Factory, in fact, is a joyful

Fig. 5.09. Moses Bridge, Fort de Roovere, Netherlands: walking on water. *Courtesy of Digital Eye*

Fig. 5.10. Solimene Factory, Italy: artificial trees shape the interior space. *Courtesy of Ceramica Artistica Solimene*

operation of bricolage, where ramps, treelike structures, terra-cotta tiles, and glass insertions create a mysterious but exuberant image. Despite its use as a factory, the design is a nod to nature and craftsmanship. Rather than seeing the factory as a purely utilitarian and alienating space, Soleri envisioned a magical world, carved into the mountain and covered by ceramics (fig. 5.10).

HYBRID EXPERIMENTS

If the Underworld is the ideal territory for exploring symbolism, irony, and metaphor, another category of Underworld architecture is driven by the use of advanced digital technologies and innovative materials—often to conserve natural resources.

Two projects designed by the Italian architect Renzo Piano at the beginning of the twenty-first century are a case in point. The Paul Klee Museum, opened in 2005 in Bern, Switzerland, is an underground space covered by a sort of rolling roof. This roof consists of three artificial hills, each with a different size, shape, and function. The first hill covers the lobby and an auditorium. The middle hill, smaller than the first, contains the permanent Klee collection. The third, smaller still, houses the research center and administrative offices. Like in one of his former projects—the California Academy of Sciences, 1998—the Paul Klee Museum blends into the surrounding landscape and challenges tradition (fig. 5.11).

In Frankfurt, German architects Schneider + Schumacher designed the extension of the Städel Museum in 2008, which holds one of the most important art collections in Europe. The new exhibition area almost doubled the original building—from 43,000 square feet to 75,000 square feet—to accommodate the entire contemporary section. This addition was one of many in the life of the museum since its construction in 1878. But this time, instead of overlaying new volumes, the architects excavated a new floor below the garden measuring 250 feet long, 170 feet wide, and 26 feet tall at its highest point.

The goal of the project was to rethink the museum's physical and metaphorical boundaries. The garden turns into a dynamic, sinuous roof of 195 circular skylights that illuminate the exhibit space below. Light intensity is scrupulously controlled through

Fig. 5.11. Paul Klee Museum, Bern: the creation of artificial topography. *Courtesy of Krol:k*

shading elements and LED systems. Moreover, the garden is no longer a simple green surface, a void that emphasized the monumental character of the old building. It now works as an extension of the interior foyer—a gathering place outside. A staircase leads visitors from the old museum to the underground space, where twelve concrete columns support the new roof and define a kind of centripetal space. Interiors are white, abstract, and filled with light. This metaphysical, suspended atmosphere is balanced by the art, which now takes center stage. Architecture steps back to emphasize the art (fig. 5.12).

In recent years, London's underground has been pressed into service to explore food culture and zero waste. In 2012, Clapham opened the first Growing Underground farm, specializing in the production of herbs and vegetables— pea shoots, rocket, red mustard, garlic, chives, coriander, and many more. This unusual farm is located in a World War II bomb shelter built a hundred feet below the ground to accommodate up to 8,000 people. Although the tunnels extend about 7,000 feet, the farm occupies only one-sixth of that space, and the plants are grown on the former bunk beds—an example of how technology becomes the interface between unconventional design, inaccessible spaces, and new programs.

In this case, plants are grown hydroponically in a pest-free environment with LED systems for light and heat, and irrigation that provides the exact amount of water and nutrients needed for each type of plant. Water can be treated on-site and recirculated, optimizing its consumption.[4]

The farm is a model for growing food where land is scarce, and a lab for experimenting with technology at a time when climate change is a global issue. Initially designed to serve a few restaurants, in the future it could feed the whole city. More important, the London underground farm is educating consumers about food culture by reconnecting them to local products, reducing food transportation and waste (fig. 5.13).

Innovation is also demonstrated in the atypical use of traditional materials. An example is the Truffle House, designed in 2010 by Ensamble Studio in Costa da Morte, Spain. Truffle House is an artificial cave meant to be ambiguous: Is it a primitive hut, military bunker, coastal observation tower? It emerges from the ground camouflaged in the natural environment. Its materials are ambiguous too: soil, concrete, and air shape a shelter that lies between the natural and the built. Its aspect is raw, violent, unfinished. But its interior is poetic, ascetic, controlled in its dimensions.

Fig. 5.12. Städel Museum, Frankfurt: view of the new garden perforated by 195 skylights. *Courtesy of Städel Museum*

Referencing Le Corbusier's Cabanon in Cap Martin, France, the Truffle is a cabin looking over the Atlantic Ocean that can just barely accommodate a bed and a table. Its construction is a synthesis of three aspects: mineral, vegetal, and animal. The first step was a hole dug in the ground and partially filled with straw bales. Concrete was poured in the hole around the bales, without structural formwork. Then, concrete and bales were covered by the excavated earth. Time passed, and when the earth was removed, an irregular mass appeared. Earth and concrete had exchanged some properties: the soil, for example, imprinted the concrete with its texture and color, and concrete gave the earth structural solidity. The animal

Fig. 5.13. Underground farm, London: the Underworld meets agricultural technology. *Courtesy of Growing Underground*

Fig. 5.14. Truffle House, Spain: interior view of the cabin. *Photo: Roland Halbe*

component of the project came from Paulina, a calf that over the course of a year ate away the straw inside the cabin, and the space's shape emerged for the first time. The next step in defining this hybrid architecture was to make it habitable. Amorphous openings became windows, and conventional components such as doors, a chimney, and furniture were introduced. By redefining how things are built, designers can transform the Underworld into an illusory space suspended between darkness and light. Plato's Allegory of the Cave touched on this same illusion, which is the starting point of any reflection about forms and ideas, knowledge and imagination, aboveground and underground (fig. 5.14).

Notes

Introduction

1. Athanasius Kircher, *Mundus subterraneus, quo universae denique naturae divitiae* (Amsterdam: Johannes Janssonius, 1665). www.archive.org/details/A149134MC/page/n8.

2. Stephen Graham, *Vertical* (Brooklyn, NY: Verso, 2016), 313.

Chapter 1

1. See Rem Koolhaas, "Elevator," in *Fundamentals: 14th International Architecture Exhibition—La Biennale di Venezia* (Venice: Marsilio, 2014).
2. Graham, *Vertical*, 369.
3. See Walter Benjamin, *Immagini di città* (Turin, Italy: Einaudi, 2007).

Chapter 2

1. See Henri Lefebvre, *The Production of Space* (London: Wiley-Blackwell, 1992).
2. Rachel Chason, "Dupont Underground Looking for Donors to Build on Initial Success," *Washington Post*, July 9, 2017. www.washingtonpost.com
3. See Eyal Weizman, *Hollow Land: Israel's Architecture of Occupation* (Brooklyn, NY: Verso, 2017).

Chapter 3

1. Bernard Rudofsky, *Architecture Without Architects: An Introduction to Non-Pedigreed Architecture* (New York: Museum of Modern Art, 1964), 10.
2. See Gideon S. Golany, *Urban Underground Space Design in China* (Newark: University of Delaware Press, 1989).
3. See Stan Allen, *Points and Lines: Diagrams and Projects for the City* (New York: Princeton Architectural Press, 1999).
4. Gabriel Samuels and Tracy You, "Inside China's Mysterious Mole-Town," *Daily Mail*, January 24, 2018. www.dailymail.co.uk /news/peoplesdaily/article-5306289/Drone-footage-shows-Chinas-mysterious-underground-village.html.
5. See Antonio Toca, *Barragan: The Complete Works* (New York: Princeton Architectural Press, 2003).
6. www.ricardobofill.com

Chapter 4

1. Dante Alighieri, *The Divine Comedy* (London: Penguin Classics, 2002), Canto XXXIV, 139.
2. See Giampiero Sanguigni, *Neutelings Riedijk* (Rome: Edilstampa, 2011).
3. See Aurelio Galfetti, *Opus 4: Castelgrande, Bellinzona* (Fellbach, Germany: Edition Axel Menges, 1992).
4. See John Pawson, *John Pawson, 1995–2005: Pausa para pensar, El Croquis* 127 (Madrid: El Croquis, 2005), 86–113.

Chapter 5

1. Johann Bernhard Fischer von Erlach, *Entwurff einer historischen Architectur* (Leipzig, 1725).
2. David Gissen, *Subnature: Architecture's Other Environments* (New York: Princeton Architectural Press, 2009).
3. Rudofsky, *Architecture Without Architects.*
4. Zlata Rodionova, "Inside London's Underground Farm," *The Independent*, February 3, 2017. www.independent.co.uk /Business/indyventure/growing-underground-london-farm-food-waste-first-food-miles-a7562151.html.

Bibliography

Ábalos, Iñaki. *2G: Lacaton & Vassal*. Barcelona: Gustavo Gili, 2012.

Alighieri, Dante. *The Divine Comedy*. London: Penguin Classics, 2002.

Allen, Stan. *Points and Lines: Diagrams and Projects for the City*. New York: Princeton Architectural Press, 1999.

Bachelard, Gaston. *The Poetics of Space*. Boston: Beacon, 1994.

Banahm, Reyner. *The Architecture of the Well-Tempered Environment*. Chicago: University of Chicago Press, 1969.

Benjamin, Walter. *Immagini di Città*. Turin, Italy: Einaudi, 2007.

Cohen, Jean-Louis. *The Future of Architecture since 1889*. London: Phaidon, 2012.

De Certeau, Michel. *The Practice of Everyday Life*. Berkeley: University of California Press, 2011.

Dobraszczyk, Paul, Carlos López Galviz, and Bradley L. Garrett, eds. *Global Undergrounds: Exploring Cities Within*. London: Reaktion Books, 2016.

Fischer von Erlach and Johann Bernhard. *Entwurff einer historischen Architektur*. Leipzig, 1725.

Galfetti, Aurelio. *Opus 4: Castelgrande, Bellinzona*. Fellbach, Germany: Edition Axel Menges, 1992.

Gissen, David. *AD: Territory. Architecture beyond Environment*. London: John Wiley & Sons, 2010.

Gissen, David. *Subnature: Architecture's Other Environments*. New York: Princeton Architectural Press, 2009.

Golany, Gideon S. *Urban Underground Space Design in China*. Newark: University of Delaware Press, 1989.

Graham, Stephen. *Vertical*. Brooklyn, NY: Verso, 2016.

Harvey, David. *A Brief History of Neoliberalism*. Oxford: Oxford University Press, 2007.

Hughes, Thomas P. *Human-Built World. How to Think about Technology and Culture*. Chicago: University of Chicago Press, 2004.

Kircher, Athanasius. *Mundus subterraneus, quo universae denique naturae divitiae*. Amsterdam: Johannes Janssonius, 1665.

Koolhaas, Rem. "Elevator." In *Fundamentals: 14th International Architecture Exhibition—La Biennale di Venezia*. Edited by Rem Koolhaas. Venice: Marsilio, 2014.

Lefebvre, Henri. *The Production of Space*. London: Wiley-Blackwell, 1992.

Meijenfeldt, Ernst Von. *Below Ground Level: Creating New Spaces for Contemporary Architecture*. Basel, Switzerland: Birkhäuser, 2002.

Olgiati, Valerio. *The Images of Architects*. Basel, Switzerland: Name Books AG, 2015.

Olgyay, Victor. *Design with Climate. Bioclimatic Approach to Architectural Regionalism*. Princeton, NJ: Princeton University Press, 2015.

Pawson, John. *John Pawson, 1995–2005: Pausa para pensar. El Croquis* 127. Madrid: El Croquis, 2005.

Pawson, John. *Minimum*. London: Phaidon, 2006.

Plato. *The Republic*. New York: Dover, 2000.

Reiser, Jesse and Nanako Umemoto. *Atlas of Novel Tectonics*. New York: Princeton Architectural Press, 2006.

Rudofsky, Bernard. *Architecture Without Architects: An Introduction to Non-Pedigreed Architecture*. New York: Museum of Modern Art, 1964.

Sanguigni, Giampiero. *Neutelings Riedijk*. Rome: Edilstampa, 2011.

Steele, James. *Architecture for People: The Complete Works of Hassan Fathy*. New York: Watson-Guptill, 1997.

Toca, Antonio. *Barragan: The Complete Works*. New York: Princeton Architectural Press, 2003.

Weizman, Eyal. *Hollow Land: Israel's Architecture of Occupation*. Brooklyn, NY: Verso, 2017.

Index

V

W

X

Y

Z

ABOUT THE AUTHOR

Stefano Corbo is an Italian architect, researcher, and assistant professor at RISD (Rhode Island School of Design). He holds a PhD and an MArch II in advanced architectural design from UPM-ETSAM Madrid (Escuela Técnica Superior de Arquitectura). Stefano has taught at several academic institutions in Europe, Asia, and the Middle East and has published two books: *From Formalism to Weak Form: The Architecture and Philosophy of Peter Eisenman* (New York: Routledge, 2014) and *Interior Landscapes: A Visual Atlas* (Mulgrave, Australia: Images, 2016). In 2012 he founded his own office, SCSTUDIO (www.scstudio.eu), a multidisciplinary network practicing public architecture and design, preoccupied with intellectual, economic, and cultural contexts.